Praise for Irshad Manji's *The Trouble with Islam*

"Her sassy but earnest perspective seems a godsend."   —*Booklist*

"[Manji's] ideas have already set off a searching debate."
—Clifford Krauss, *The New York Times*

"What is most moving about Manji's testament is…her refreshing vision of a modern, communally vital but nonexclusionary Islam."   —*Elle*

"Such questioning is refreshingly provocative…*The Trouble with Islam* deserves the attention it is receiving."   —*The Wall Street Journal*

"Her book will be an unsettling read for most of her fellow Muslims, although they may find themselves agreeing with many points."
—*Publishers Weekly*

"Feisty and fearless."   —*The Economist*

"[E]ngaging and lively…[B]igger, much bigger, than girl meets God."
—*O, The Oprah Magazine* (May 2004)

"Manji—a practicing Muslim—brings real insight to her subject."
—Daniel Pipes, *New York Post*

"Irshad Manji has written a bold, sane, passionate, and compelling book that should earn it praise and attention. Despite the seriousness of its subject, the book is easy to understand and quite enjoyable to read."
—Phyllis Chesler, Ph.D., Emerita Professor of Psychology and Women's Studies, and the author of *Women and Madness* and *The New Anti-Semitism: The Current Crisis and What We Must Do About It*

"Irshad Manji is a fresh, new, and intriguing voice of Islamic reform. This wonderfully written book will surprise you, educate you, even entertain you."   — Alan Dershowitz, author of *The Case for Israel*

"*The Trouble with Islam* is beyond controversial. It may ignite a firestorm of protest…her easy conversational style, addressed to 'my fellow Muslims,' makes it accessible to a wide range of readers."
—Leslie Scrivener, *The Toronto Star*

"Irshad Manji has written a book that tests the aphorism 'the pen is mightier than the sword.'…timely and important…challenges the reader to ask questions and think."   —Shehani Kay, *Winnipeg Free Press*

THE TROUBLE WITH ISLAM TODAY

THE TROUBLE
WITH
ISLAM
TODAY

A Muslim's Call for Reform in Her Faith

Irshad Manji

ST. MARTIN'S GRIFFIN ✿ NEW YORK

www.stmartins.com

Library of Congress Cataloging-in-Publication Data

Manji, Irshad.
    The trouble with Islam today : a Muslim's call for reform in her faith / Irshad Manji.
        p. cm
    Includes bibliographical references (p. 219).
    ISBN 0-312-32699-8 (hc)
    ISBN 0-312-32700-5 (pbk)
    EAN 978-0312-32700-2
    1. Islam—Controversial literature.   2. Islam and civil society.
3. Liberty of conscience (Islam).   4. Islam—Essence, genius, nature.
I. Title.

BP169.M28 2003
297—dc22

                                                                2003058188

First published in Canada by Random House Canada

10 9 8 7 6 5 4 3 2

To my grandmother, Laila Nasser,
who asks great questions when given the chance,
and to the many individual Muslims
who have already taken chances

CONTENTS

PROLOGUE

Let us face a simple fact: I should hate Irshad Manji. If Muslims listen to her, they will stop listening to people like me, an imam who spent years at a traditional Islamic university.

She threatens my male authority and says things about Islam that I wish were not true. She has a big mouth, and fact upon fact to corroborate her analysis. She doesn't fear death, except the kind that comes from shutting down one's brain. She is a lesbian, and my *madressa* training has instilled, almost into my DNA, that Allah hates gays and lesbians. I really should hate this woman.

But then I look into my heart and engage my mind, and I come to a discomfiting conclusion: Irshad is telling the truth. And my God commands me to uphold the truth—which means that I have to side with her.

However, that is not why I write this prologue. I do so because I need to atone for acting like a hypocrite.

I am often commended for my bravery in opposing extremist Islam and terrorism. I can't downplay the accolades because it does demand a certain amount of courage to do what I do. It should therefore not have required a colossal sacrifice of testosterone to defend Irshad when she needed it.

Recently, I had that opportunity, and I failed to take it. I'd just come home from a conference, where I'd stirred a flap by urging Muslims to move beyond anti-Semitism. Some Muslims decided to do the right thing: They met with me to determine exactly what I'd said. In the course of the discussion, someone brought up Irshad's name. The group derided her as a little lesbian troublemaker. And there I sat like a gutted chicken, mute and unmoving, not wanting to take on yet another issue. I, the man, the "upholder and protector" of women, deemed to be so by divine mandate in a seventh-century document that the madrassa teachers told me is for all time, I could not utter a word.

That is when I realized that all this nonsense had to stop. Am I a Muslim or am I not? Do I care for truth or do I not? This is why I now declare, not just for those Muslims who met with me, but for all Muslims everywhere: I support Irshad Manji. She wants us to do what our Holy Book wants us to do: End the tribal posturing, open our eyes, and stand up to oppression, even if it's rationalized by our vaunted imams, sheikhs, mullahs, professors, and whatever other titles the packagers of Islam give themselves.

Rarely, if ever, has a Muslim stated publicly what so many of us know but dare not confirm. Irshad pulls no punches as she exposes Jew-bashing, as well as the urge to lay the responsibility for all of Islam's ills on Western colonization, while neglecting Islam's own history of imperialism and continued human rights abuses in the name of Allah. Throughout her book, Irshad remains obedient to the Divine Imperative: "O you who believe! Be upholders of justice, witnesses for God, even if it be against yourselves, or your parents and kin. . . ." (Quran, 4:135)

While obeying Allah, Irshad beats the mullahs at their own game. One of the most onerous prerequisites of *ijtihad,* Islam's tradition of independent reasoning, is that one be familiar with all the latest thinkers in Islam. On this score, Irshad is way ahead of many clerics. In fact, her book can serve as a primer on the views of modern Muslim intellectuals. Where else can one find such an astute analysis of Sa'd el-Din Ibrahim, Mahmoud Taha, Khaled Abou El-Fadl, Nasr Abu Zayd, and several others?

To be sure, Irshad has opened herself up to criticism by choosing a defiantly democratic form of expression—the book as an open letter. This approach dents the egos of the elite because she refuses to write strictly for us and our clubby constituents. Irshad's work does not fall into the typology of academic theories couched in almost incomprehensible ivory-tower jargon. Nor does it represent the usual romantic ode to Islam that holds meaning only to a follower. Instead, Irshad's honesty, style, and clarity catapult the book into a class by itself.

You, the reader, may not agree with all of Irshad's conclusions. I certainly don't. But this is precisely her goal. To expect any different would be to defeat the very freedom of thought that she seeks to reintroduce in Islam.

—*Dr. Khaleel Mohammed*
San Diego State University

Dr. Khaleel Mohammed teaches religion at San Diego State University. He is also an imam who studied at the Kulliyat al-Shariah, Muhammad bin Saud University, in Riyadh. His responsa can be found at www.forpeoplewhothink.org

THE LETTER

"Believers: Conduct yourselves with justice and bear true witness, even if it be against yourselves, your parents, or your kin."

(Koran 4:135)

My Fellow Muslims,

I have to be honest with you. Islam is on very thin ice with me. I'm hanging on by my fingernails, in anxiety over what's coming next from the self-appointed ambassadors of Allah.

When I consider all the fatwas being hurled by the brain trust of our faith, I feel utter embarrassment. Don't you? I hear from a Saudi friend that his country's religious police arrest women for wearing red on Valentine's Day, and I think: Since when does a merciful God outlaw joy—or fun?* I read about victims of rape being stoned for "adultery," and I wonder how a critical mass of us can stay stone silent.

When non-Muslims beg us to speak up, I hear you gripe that we shouldn't have to explain the behavior of other Muslims. Yet when we're misunderstood, we fail to see that it's precisely because

---

*All claims are substantiated by source notes on my Web site. Please visit www.muslim-refusenik.com.

we haven't given people a reason to think differently about us. On top of that, when I speak publicly about our failings, the very Muslims who detect stereotyping at every turn then stereotype me as a sellout. A sellout to what? To moral clarity? To common decency? To civilization?

Yes, I'm blunt. You're just going to have to get used to it. In this letter, I'm asking questions from which we can no longer hide. Why are we all being held hostage by what's happening between the Palestinians and the Israelis? What's with the stubborn streak of anti-Semitism in Islam? Who is the real colonizer of Muslims—America or Arabia? Why are we squandering the talents of women, fully half of God's creation? How can we be so sure that homosexuals deserve ostracism—or death—when the Koran states that everything God made is "excellent"? Of course, the Koran states more than that, but what's our excuse for reading the Koran literally when it's so contradictory and ambiguous?

Is that a heart attack you're having? Make it fast. Because if we don't speak out against the imperialists within Islam, these guys will walk away with the show. And their path leads to a dead end of more vitriol, more violence, more poverty, more exclusion. Is this the justice we seek for the world that God has leased to us? If it's not, then why don't more of us say so publicly?

What I do hear from you is that Muslims are the targets of backlash. In France, Muslims have actually taken an author to court for calling Islam "the most stupid religion." Apparently, he's inciting hate. So we assert our rights—something most of us wouldn't have in Islamic countries. But is the French guy wrong to write that Islam needs to grow up? What about the Koran's incitement of hate against Jews? Shouldn't Muslims who invoke the Koran to justify anti-Semitism be themselves open to a lawsuit? Or would this amount to more "backlash"? What makes us righteous and everybody else racist?

Through our screaming self-pity and our conspicuous silences, we Muslims are conspiring against ourselves. We're in crisis, and we're dragging the rest of the world with us. If ever there was a moment for an Islamic reformation, it's now. For the love of God, what are we doing about it?

You may wonder who I am to talk to you this way. I am a Muslim Refusenik. That doesn't mean I refuse to be a Muslim; it simply means I refuse to join an army of automatons in the name of Allah. I take this phrase from the original refuseniks—Soviet Jews who championed religious and personal freedom. Their communist masters refused to let them emigrate to Israel. For their attempts to leave the Soviet Union, many refuseniks paid with hard labor and, sometimes, with their lives. Over time, though, their persistent refusal to comply with the mechanisms of mind control and soullessness helped end a totalitarian system.

Likewise, I tip my hat to the newer refuseniks—Israeli soldiers who protest the military occupation of the West Bank and Gaza. In the same spirit of conscientious dissent, we've got to protest the ideological occupation of Muslim minds. The trouble with Islam today is that literalism is going mainstream, worldwide.

You'll want to assure me that what I'm describing isn't "true" Islam. I hope you're right. That's why I'm writing this open letter—because I believe that we Muslims *are* capable of being more thoughtful and humane than most of our clerics give us credit for. But for the sake of an honest discussion, I have to challenge you to come clean about the Islam that you reflexively defend. Is this Islam in its real form or Islam as an ideal? Let's face it, everything is wonderful as an ideal. Communism is egalitarian as an ideal. Capitalism is fair as an ideal. The United States Constitution guarantees liberty and justice for all, as an ideal. Muslims know that the reality is very different. As people of conscience, we have to address Islam's realities too.

I think Prophet Muhammad would have embraced this distinction between the real and the ideal. When he was asked to define religion, he reportedly replied that religion is the way we conduct ourselves toward others. A fine definition—simple without being simplistic. And yet, by that definition, how we Muslims behave, not in theory but in actuality, *is* Islam. Which means our complacency is Islam. It also means the power is ours to restore Islam's better angels, those who care about the human rights of women and religious minorities. To do that, though, we have to snap out of our denial. By insisting that there's nothing the matter with Islam, we're sweeping the reality of our religion today under the rug of Islam as an ideal, thereby absolving ourselves of responsibility for our fellow human beings, including our fellow Muslims. See why I'm struggling?

By writing this open letter, I'm not implying that other religions are problem-free. Hardly. The difference is, libraries abound in books about the trouble with Christianity. There's no shortage of books about the trouble with Judaism. We Muslims have a lot of catching up to do in the dissent department.

Whose permission are we waiting for?

1

HOW I BECAME
A MUSLIM REFUSENIK

Like millions of Muslims over the last forty years, my family immigrated to the West. We arrived in Richmond, a middle-class suburb of Vancouver, British Columbia, in 1972. I was four years old. Between 1971 and 1973, thousands of South Asian Muslims fled Uganda after the military dictator, General Idi Amin Dada, proclaimed Africa to be for the blacks. He gave those of us with brown skin mere weeks to leave or we would die. Muslims had spent lifetimes in East Africa thanks to the British, who brought us from South Asia to help lay the railways in their African colonies. Within a few generations, many Muslims rose to the rank of well-off merchants. My father and his brothers ran a Mercedes-Benz dealership near Kampala, benefiting from the class mobility that the British bequeathed to us but that we, in turn, rarely granted to the native blacks whom we employed.

In the main, the Muslims of East Africa treated blacks like slaves. I remember my father beating Tomasi, our domestic, hard enough to raise shiny bruises on his pitch-dark limbs. Although my two sisters, my mother, and I loved Tomasi, we too would be pummeled if my dad caught us tending to his injuries. I knew this to be happening in many more Muslim households than mine, and the bondage continued well after my family left. That's why, as a teenager, I turned down the opportunity to visit relatives in East Africa. "If I go with you," I warned my mother, "you know I'll have to ask your fat aunties and uncles why they practically enslave their servants." Mum meant the trip to be a good-bye to aging relations, not a human rights campaign. In order to avoid embarrassing her, I stayed home.

While Mum was away, I thought more about what it means be "home." I decided that home is where my dignity lives, not necessarily where my ancestors put down roots. That's when it dawned on me why the postcolonial fever of pan-Africanism— "Africa for the blacks!"—swept the continent on which I was born. Many Muslims made dignity difficult for people darker than us. We callously exploited native Africans. And please don't tell me that we learned colonial ruthlessness from the British because that begs the question: Why didn't we also learn to make room for entrepreneurial blacks as the Brits had made room for us?

I don't apologize for being offended by the notion of having a Tomasi. Most of you, I'm sure, oppose servitude, too. But it wasn't Islam that fostered my belief in the dignity of every individual. It was the democratic environment to which my family and I migrated: Richmond, where even a little Muslim girl can be engaged—and I don't mean for marriage. Let me explain.

A couple of years after the family settled down, my dad discovered free baby-sitting services at Rose of Sharon Baptist Church. (Say "free" to an immigrant and religious affiliations take a backseat to the bargain at hand.) Every week, when Mum left the house to sell Avon products door to door, my less-than-child-friendly father dumped the kids at church. There, the South Asian lady who supervised Bible study showed me and my older sister the same patience she displayed with her own son. She made me believe my questions were worth asking. Obviously, the questions I posed as a seven-year-old could only be simple ones. Where did Jesus come from? When did he live? What was his job? Who did he marry? These queries didn't put anyone on the spot, but my point is that the act of asking—and asking some more—always met with an inviting smile.

Maybe that's what motivated me, at age eight, to win the Most Promising Christian of the Year Award. My prize: a brightly illustrated edition of *101 Bible Stories*. I look back now and thank God I wound up in a world where the Koran didn't have to be my first and only book, as if it's the lone richness that life offers to believers. Besides, *101 Bible Stories* riveted me with its pictures. What would *101 Koran Stories* look like? At the time, I hadn't seen such a thing. Today, there's no dearth of children's books about Islam, including *A Is for Allah,* by Yusuf Islam (formerly Cat Stevens). Free societies allow for the reinvention of self and the evolution of faiths.

Shortly after I earned the title of Most Promising Christian, Dad plucked me out of the church. A *madressa,* or Islamic religious school, would soon be constructed. This little geek couldn't wait. If my Sunday school experience was any barometer, the madressa would be fun, or so I innocently assumed.

Meanwhile, my new world was growing up with me. A sprawling mall that would be pivotal in my education as a Muslim, Lansdowne Centre, opened. The names of Richmond's founding Scots, emblazoned on outdoor signs—Brighouse,

McNair, Burnett, Steveston—soon jostled for attention with words in Hindi, Punjabi, Urdu, Mandarin, Cantonese, Korean, and Japanese. These languages blanketed the interior of Aberdeen Centre, built several years later and billed as "the largest enclosed Asian-themed shopping plaza in North America."

Well before then, it struck me that a place like Richmond could accommodate just about anybody who expressed initiative. In the tenth grade, I ran for student body president at J. N. Burnett Junior High School. The year before, I'd lost my bid to become homeroom representative, the deciding vote being cast by a grungy twerp who didn't want a "Paki" in charge of his classroom. Only a year later, a majority of students in the whole school made this Paki their duly elected leader. In Richmond, racism didn't have to fence my ambitions any more than race itself had to define me.

A few months after I became student body president, the vice-principal of my school was strolling past my locker and stopped dead when he glimpsed the poster of Iranian revolutionaries I had taped inside. Sent to me by an uncle in France, the poster depicted women in black *chadors* smashing the wings of an airplane. The left wing had the Soviet hammer and sickle painted on it and the right wing sported the U.S. stars and stripes.

"This isn't appropriate," he cautioned me. "Take it down."

I pointed to the next locker over, whose door had an American flag hanging from it. "If she can express her opinion openly," I asked, "why can't I?"

"Because you're trivializing our democratic values. And as president of all students, you should know better."

I confess to not realizing that Ayatollah Khomeini's regime oozed totalitarianism. I hadn't done my homework. Seduced partly by propaganda and partly by the pride of living in a free society, I wanted to advocate diversity of opinion so that the Star-Spangled Banner wouldn't strangle other perspectives. So I argued. "I'm trivializing democracy? How is it that you're supporting democracy by telling me that I can't express myself, but," pointing to the flag-draped locker, "somebody else can?"

We stared at each other. "You're setting a bad example," the vice-principal said. He stiffened his back and walked away.

You've got to credit him for letting diversity of opinion survive at Burnett Junior High. It's all the more admirable given his own embrace of evangelical Christianity. He didn't veil his personal beliefs, but neither did he foist them on the students—not when the student council president appeared to be a booster of Khomeini's theocracy, and not even when the students lobbied for school shorts that revealed more leg than our vice-principal thought reasonable. After a heated debate with us and a few strategic delays, he okayed the shorts, bristling but still respecting popular will. How many Muslim evangelicals do you know who tolerate the expression of viewpoints that distress their souls? Of course, my vice-principal had to bite his tongue in the public school system, but such a system can only emerge from a consensus that people of different faiths, backgrounds, aspirations, and stations ought to tussle together. How many Muslim countries tolerate such a tussle?

Lord, I loved this society. I loved that it seemed perpetually unfinished, the final answers not yet known—if ever they would be. I loved that, in a world under constant renovation, the contributions of individuals mattered.

But at home, my father's ready fist ensured his family's obedience to an arbitrary domestic drill. *Don't laugh at dinner. When I steal your savings, shut up. When I kick your ass, remember, it'll be harder next time. When I pound your mother, don't call the police. If they show up, I'll charm them into leaving, and you know they will. The moment they're gone, I'll slice off your ear. If you threaten to alert social services, I'll amputate your other ear.*

The one time my father chased me through the house with a knife, I managed to fly out of my bedroom window and spend the night on the roof. My mum had no idea of my situation because she was working the graveyard shift at an airline company. Just as well; I'm not sure I would have crawled down for any promise of safety she might have offered. For the same reason that I liked my school and Rose of Sharon Baptist Church and, years later, Aberdeen Centre, I liked the roof. From each of these perches, I could survey a world of open-ended possibility. In the East African Muslim community from which I came, would I have been allowed to dream of a formal education? Of landing scholarships? Of participating in political races, never mind holding office? To judge by the grainy black-and-white photos that showed me, at age three, playing a bride with her head covered, hands folded, eyes downcast, and legs dangling from the sofa, I can only guess that unremitting subservience would have been my lot if we'd stayed in the confines of Muslim Uganda. How's that for a firm grasp of the obvious?

The bigger question is this: Why did the Richmond madressa, set up by immigrants to this land of rights and freedoms, choose autocracy? From age nine to age fourteen, I spent every Saturday there. Classes took place on the upper floor of the newly built mosque, which resembled a mammoth suburban house more than it did Middle Eastern architecture. Inside, however, you got stern Islam through and through. Men and women entered the mosque by different doors and planted themselves on the correct sides of an immovable wall that cut the building in half, quarantining the sexes during worship. Set in this wall was a door that connected the men's and women's sides. This came in handy after services, when men would demand more food from the communal kitchen by thrusting their bowls through the door, banging on the wall, and waiting mere seconds for a woman's arm to thrust back the replenished bowls. In the mosque, men never had to see women, and women never had to be seen. If that isn't the definition of assigning us small lives, then I'm missing something big.

One flight up was the madressa, with its depressing decor of burnt-brown rugs, fluorescent lights, and portable partitions that separated the girls from the boys. Wherever classes congregated within the wide expanse of that room, a partition would tag along. Worse was the partition between mind and soul. In my Saturday classes I learned that if you're spiritual, you don't think. If you think, you're not spiritual. This facile equation rubbed up against the exhilarating curiosity in me that Richmond indulged. Call it my personal clash of civilizations.

The solution wasn't simply to accept that there's a secular world and a nonsecular one, and that each has its ways of being. By that logic, the decidedly nonsecular Rose of Sharon Baptist Church should have quashed my questions. Instead, my curiosity brought me praise there. At Burnett Junior High, a secular school, my questions bugged the bejeezus out of my vice-principal but nobody shut me down. In both places, the dignity of the individual prevailed. Not so at my madressa. I entered its premises wearing a white polyester chador and departed several hours later with my hair flattened and my spirit deflated, as if the condom over my head had properly inoculated me from "unsafe" intellectual activity.

Before airing more dirty laundry, let me be fair to my

madressa teacher—we'll call him Mr. Khaki. He was as sincere a Muslim as they come. This bony brother with a finely trimmed beard (signifying cleanliness) and a Honda Mini Compact (indicating modesty) volunteered his services each weekend (proving charity) to give the children of Muslim immigrants the religious education that they might otherwise forfeit to the promiscuity of values in a multicultural country. No easy task, since the madressa attracted students from across the age spectrum: self-conscious prepubescents struggling with acne, giggly types who took cover in the bathroom, adolescents sprouting moustaches—and that's just the girls. I'm kidding . . . sort of.

Most of us saw the madressa not so much as a place of learning, but as a pond from which to fish out our future mates. Because mouthy chicks don't get husbands, my girlfriends rarely argued with Mr. Khaki. So what was my problem? Didn't I want to be somebody's wife someday? Don't get me started. My problem was this: Enamored of that multilayered world beyond the madressa, I insisted on being educated rather than indoctrinated.

The trouble began with *Know Your Islam,* the primer that I packed in my madressa bag every week. After reading it, I needed to know more about "my" Islam. Why must girls observe the essentials, such as praying five times a day, at an earlier age than boys? Because, Mr. Khaki told me, girls mature sooner. They reach the "obligatory age" of practice at nine compared to thirteen for boys.

"Then why not reward girls for our maturity by letting us lead prayer?" I asked.

"Girls can't lead prayer."

"What do you mean?"

"Girls aren't permitted."

"Why not?"

"Allah says so."

"What's His reason?"

"Read the Koran."

I tried, though it felt artificial since I didn't know Arabic. Do I see you nodding your head? Most Muslims have no clue what we're saying when we're reciting the Koran in Arabic. It's not that we're obtuse. Rather, Arabic is one of the world's most rhythmic languages, and weekly lessons at the madressa simply don't let us grasp its intricacies. *Haram,* for instance, can refer to something forbidden or something sacred, depending on which "a" you stress. Forbidden versus sacred: We're not talking subtle shifts in meaning here. To the inherent challenges of this language, add the realities of life. In my case, a violent father who practiced religion mostly for show and a mother who did her best to be devout while striving to sustain a household on shift work. You can appreciate why Arabic study failed to rate as a family priority. Frankly, Mr. Khaki's stock reply to my questions—"Read the Koran"—fell about as flat as my chador-chastened hair.

Over time, this read-the-Koran response generated more questions: Why should I perpetuate the fib of reciting Arabic if it makes no practical sense and strikes no emotional chord? Why must we suspect that every English translation of the Koran "corrupts" the original text? I mean, if the Koran is as straightforward as the purists tell us, then aren't its teachings easily translated into a thousand tongues? Finally, why should stigma stalk those of us who haven't been weaned on Arabic when the fact is that no more than 20 percent of Muslims worldwide are Arabs? Translation: At least 80 percent of us aren't Arabs. "Know Your Islam," they say blithely. Whose Islam? Is this a faith or a cult?

All right, time-out.

Let's pick up my original question to Mr. Khaki: Why can't girls lead prayer? Figuring that the Koran's answer would be repeated in some other book I might have a prayer of under-standing, I attempted to access the madressa's library. What a production to arrange that trip. The library was a series of racks situated at the top of the stairs on the men's side of the mosque—off-limits to ladies without advance approval. Being eleven years old and of "obligatory age," I couldn't consort with adult males. So I had to persuade a boy under the obliga-tory age—twelve or younger—to run upstairs on my behalf and secure permission for me any time I wanted to browse. Assum-ing I got the green light, all the men had to clear the area before I could ascend the stairs and pick through the collection of cheap brochures in the racks. Of course, my time was severely restricted since the men were waiting to return to their space. I managed to borrow a few pamphlets each time, but their con-tents were so hard to follow, I don't know where their authors went to school. Two years of getting the runaround inside the mosque proved fruitless. At thirteen, I realized that I'd have to circumvent Mr. Khaki and the madressa in order to have my question addressed.

I became a mall-rat. My mission? To track down an English-language Koran. Lansdowne Centre delivered, may God bless my town's bazaar of beliefs. Freedom of information might have frightened Mr. Khaki, but it was exactly this freedom that allowed one of his students to find more meaning in her religion—a meaning the madressa wouldn't supply.

What did I learn about why girls can't lead prayer? I can't tell you right now. Because even if mullahs and madressa teachers supply pat answers, the Koran doesn't. What I can tell you is that in between elections, drama rehearsals, part-time jobs, volleyball practices—up to, into, and beyond university—I made my way through the scripture with the "woman question" top of mind. I'm still reading. To divulge my conclusions at this point would be to leapfrog into my adult life. First, I have to deal with something else.

The Jews. It's the other question that perturbed me during my madressa years because the Jews came in for a regular tarring. Mr. Khaki taught us with a straight face that Jews worship moolah, not Allah, and that their idolatry would pollute my piety if I hung out with them. What planet, I wondered, did Mr. Khaki inhabit? Was he willfully blind to our surroundings? Richmond, a below-sea-level suburb, was more likely to drown in Asian commercial influence than to become submerged by any mountain of money the Jews could stockpile. If Richmond had even one synagogue at the time, I didn't know about it.

Then again, maybe I was an agent of their shadowy power, because I certainly managed to disrupt Mr. Khaki's passionate history lessons with questions about Jews. I remember asking why Prophet Muhammad would have commanded his army to kill an entire Jewish tribe when the Koran supposedly came to him as a message of peace. Mr. Khaki couldn't cope. He shot me a look of contempt, gave an annoyed wave of the hand, and cut short history class, only to hold Koran study next. Me and my big mouth.

A year after I bought my English-language Koran, Mr. Khaki and I reached an impasse. Nothing I had read so far convinced me of a Jewish conspiracy. Granted, a year is scarcely enough time to digest the Koran and, at fourteen, there's a lot of mental maturing still to do. I couldn't quite brush off Mr. Khaki's anti-Semitic harangues. Who was I to decide he was full of bunk until I had all the evidence? So I challenged him to provide proof of the Jewish plot. What he provided was an ultimatum: Either you believe or get out. And if you get out, get out for good.

Really? That's it?

That's it.

With my temples throbbing and my neck sweating under the itchy polyester chador, I stood up. As I crossed the partition checkpoint, I could have uncovered my head for all the boys to see, but I didn't want to risk the humiliation of being chased out by an even more scandalized Mr. Khaki. All I could think to do was fling open the madressa's hefty metal door and yell, "Jesus Christ!" A memorable exit, I hoped. Only later would I realize just how memorable. Jesus was a Jew!

ARE YOU WONDERING WHY, AFTER MY EXPULSION FROM THE madressa, I didn't damn the whole religion and get on with celebrating my "emancipated" North American self? In part, the imperative of identity kicked in. You know what I'm driving at. Most of us Muslims aren't Muslims because we think about it, but rather because we're born that way. It's "who we are."

My madressa meltdown embarrassed my mum, yet she'd lived with me too long to believe she could order me to grovel for Mr. Khaki's forgiveness. Not a chance. Nor did she force me to go to mosque with her. For a couple of years, though, I actually did. It was the one place that remained open to me on the map of my fragile Muslim-hood. I loved God, and I wasn't about to punish the mosque for the sins of the madressa—until it gradually sank in that the madressa I loathed was an extension of the mosque. Attending the mosque might have allowed me to identify as a Muslim, but it also obliged me to sacrifice that other, equally sacred, part of my identity: thinker.

Let me tell you another story. Among Islam's five pillars is charity. So, a buzz of approval permeated the air one evening when the loudspeaker on the women's side of the mosque, blaring the voice of the mullah on the men's side of the mosque, announced a drive to raise money for our Muslim brothers and sisters overseas. We were to have our checks ready in a few days. During that interval, I asked a member of the ladies' auxiliary where the money would be sent. She mentioned an Islamic organization with a clunky name. I asked her what the funds would be used for. To feed our fellow Muslims, she replied. Recalling TV news stories about fraud charges against Christian charities, I asked how we'd know that the money would end up where we intended. "It's going to Muslims," she snapped. "That's all you need to know."

Do you buy it? I didn't. My quarrel wasn't with alms-giving but with information-hoarding. Why should I rest easy merely because people who call themselves Muslims will have my donation? Is it that by virtue of being a Muslim, every Muslim is, well, virtuous? Talk about faith. Where was the crime in my queries? Or were the queries themselves the crime? My beleaguered mother didn't appear altogether shocked when I explained that I couldn't add to the family's donation because, really, who cares what religion a hungry person is, and besides, I was wary about the scheme being sold to us. Instead, I said, my alms would go to a nonreligious charity whose credentials I would research.

The more the mosque felt like the madressa, the less I attended. I started to decentralize my faith, cultivating a personal relationship with God rather than assuming it had to be mediated through a congregation. In that spirit, I prayed in solitude ("bowing alone," as the Harvard sociologist, Robert Putnam, might say). Every day for years, I'd wake up early and shiver my way into an unheated bathroom—my refugee mother believed in low bills as much as in a higher power. After washing my feet, arms, and face, I'd unfurl my velvet rug in the hallway, position it toward Mecca, lay down the piece of Arabian clay that my forehead would touch, and spend the next ten minutes praying. It's a discipline-building exercise, especially since you cleanse yourself two more times a day, and utter four more sets of prayers.

Still, the entire exercise of washing prescribed parts of the body, reciting specified verses, and prostrating at a nonnegotiable angle, all at assigned times of the day, can degenerate into mindless submission—and habitual submissiveness. If you haven't seen this tendency in your parents or grandparents, you're some rare Muslim, my friend. I realized that what began as a guide to godliness had become rote, compelling me to replace my prayer "routine" with something more self-aware: candid, unstructured conversations with my Creator throughout the day. It may sound flaky, but at least I can say those words were my own.

It wouldn't have been a much greater leap at that point to renounce Islam wholesale and walk away from my Muslim identity. You know what stopped me? A devotion to fairness. I've always believed in giving Islam a fair shake because, to my Western sensibility, merit ought to matter. I needed to discover Islam's personality instead of its posturing. An analogy: When I was thirteen or so, my mother urged me to make nice with an obnoxious cousin. "She's family," Mum reasoned. "She's our blood." I retorted that blood meant nothing to me. The relevant question was whether I would choose to be her friend at school if we weren't related. With a personality like that, forget it. To expend energy "liking" my cousin would be a charade, and I had better things to do with my time. Although Mum understood, she didn't agree. For her, family took precedence. For me, lineage didn't equal merit. Personality did.

I brought the same standard to religion. In order to decide whether I should practice Islam, I had to discover its merits—or lack of them. And I had to discover this for myself, replacing the mosque and its programmed pieties with my own quest for the personality of Islam. Maybe the Koran really does dehumanize Jews and subjugate women. Or maybe Mr. Khaki was a lousy teacher. Maybe God commands that everyone speak Arabic. Or maybe that's a manmade rule to keep most Muslims dependent on higher-ups. Maybe diverging from the spiritual script insults the Almighty. Or maybe we pay tribute to Allah's creative powers when we use our own. I didn't know. But without exploring the alternative, walking away would have felt like running away.

The good news is I knew I lived in a part of the world that permitted me to explore. Thanks to the freedoms afforded me in the West—to think, search, speak, exchange, discuss, challenge, be challenged, and rethink—I was poised to judge my religion in a light that I couldn't have possibly conceived in the parochial Muslim microcosm of the madressa. No need to choose between Islam and the West. On the contrary, the West made it possible for me to choose Islam, however tentatively. It was up to Islam to retain me.

I DIDN'T OBSESS ABOUT RELIGION, BUT EVERY NOW AND AGAIN A question would pop up, and I hunted for answers in the only place I thought might have some. Picture it: The public library in the pre-Internet period of the 1980s and early 1990s. Most of what I'd read about Islam exuded a textbook tone. Lots of reference, little risk. Then, on February 14, 1989, Iran's Ayatollah

Khomeini declared a fatwa against Salman Rushdie, author of *The Satanic Verses*. This "unfunny Valentine," as Rushdie would later call the fatwa, demanded of Westerners more than a collective tiptoe around theocracy. Many people in the West did take a stand against the death warrant and I'd be disingenuous to deny that. But the commentaries I tracked down at the public library seemed satisfied with merely explaining Muslim outrage; they steered away from asking if the Koran is as virgin, as divine, as the effigy-burners would have us believe. What happened to the religiously respectful yet intellectually messy West I'd fallen in love with? Was multiculturalism losing its mind?

In a crucial sense, I think so. I say this because my trips to the library coincided with the era of Edward Said. He was the Arab-American intellectual who, in 1979, used the word *Orientalism* to describe the West's supposed tendency to colonize Muslims by demonizing them as exotic freaks of the East. A compelling theory, but doesn't it speak volumes that the "imperialist" West published, distributed, and promoted Edward Said's book?

Within a decade, Said was all the rage among young academics-turned-activists in North America and Europe. Their worship of him effectively stifled other ideas about Islam. By the time Salman Rushdie came out with *The Satanic Verses*, Said's acolytes stood ready to denounce as "Orientalist" (read: racist) just about anything that affronted mainstream Muslims. In my experience, the public library didn't escape this chill.

I began to regain faith, in both the West and Islam, after the mid-1990s. Praise Allah for the Internet. With the Web making self-censorship irrelevant—someone else is bound to say what you won't—it became the place where intellectual risk-takers finally exhaled. They reasserted what makes the West a fierce if imperfect incubator of ideas: its love of discovery, including discovery of its own biases. And as the critics probed Islam, I picked up on some jaw-dropping aspects of my religion.

How many of us know the degree to which Islam is a "gift of the Jews"? The unity of God's creation, the inherent and often mysterious justice of God, our innate capacity, as God's creatures, to choose good, the purposefulness of our earthly lives, the infinity of the afterlife—these and other biggies of monotheism came to Muslims via Judaism. This discovery astounded me because it suggested that Muslims need not be steeped in anti-Semitism. If anything, we have reason to be grateful rather than hateful to Jews.

Nor, until educating myself, did I appreciate that Muslims worship exactly the same God as do the Jews and the Christians. The Koran affirms this fact. Truth is, though, I had to read a recent book by the British religious scholar Karen Armstrong before that point penetrated my madressa-molded mind. (What can I tell you? Deprogramming is a many-splendored thing.) Armstrong emphasizes that Prophet Muhammad didn't claim to introduce a new God to the entire world. His personal mission was to bring Arabs into the "rightly guided" family of Abraham, the first prophet to receive the revelation that there's one sovereign God. Growing up, I never heard Abraham's name in a history lesson. A glaring omission, given that Abraham's progeny went on to found the Jewish nation. Being the debut monotheists, the Jews laid the groundwork for the Christians and, later, the Muslims to emerge. So, you see, Muslims didn't invent one God; they renamed Him Allah. That's Arabic for "The God"— the God of Jews and Christians.

Where in the madressa curriculum was that acknowledgment? It's as if nothing happened before Islam. Yet, if all pre-Islamic experience counts for naught, then so must a slew of our principles as Muslims. If more of us knew that Islam is the product of intermingling histories, as opposed to a wholly original way of life—if we understood that we're spiritual mongrels—would more of us be willing to accept the "other"? I began to wonder why we're so reluctant to acknowledge outside influences, except when blaming the West for assorted colonial injuries. Which, in turn, raised a fundamental question: Is Islam more narrow-minded than the rest of the world's religions?

There's a party-wrecker of a topic. From university on, whenever people did agree to a discussion about Islam's intolerant bent, they would caution me not to confuse religion with culture. "Stoning women has everything to do with tribal customs and nothing to do with Islam," tutored one woman at a dinner. I remained a skeptic. If Islam is flexible, then it can adapt for good and not only for ill, right? So why didn't anything about my mosque resemble Richmond's democracy—the very democracy that allowed Muslims to erect a mosque there?

It wasn't just the modern Muslim in me who had to wrestle with these issues. My career as a TV journalist and commentator placed me on the front line of the public's own questions about Islam. Having seen my face in their living rooms, average folks feel no hesitation about approaching me in shops, restaurants, and subway cars to voice a basic concern: If you're going to be a beard-busting, chador-defying Muslim, God help and save you. But as long you choose to stick with Islam, how do you account for so much bigotry under its banner? More precisely, they've asked, "Are you allowed to be a Muslim and a feminist?" "What does it take to turn a devout Muslim into a suicide bomber?" "Why aren't more Muslims speaking up?" "Aren't you afraid to speak up?" And, "How come I've never heard a joke about a priest, a rabbi, and a mullah?" Since getting hit with that last stumper, I've done some serious digging, and I think I've gained an insight. Permit me a quick diversion.

Islam has a popular teaching against "excessive laughter." No joke. In a booklet titled *Problems and Solutions*, Sheikh Muhammed Salih Al-Munajjid spells out the teaching. While "the Muslim is not expected to be dour-faced," an abundance of laughter proves that we Muslims have been manipulated by charm and wit, which softens our character and piety. I recall an uncle lovingly but firmly warning me one New Year's Eve not to laugh too hard as doom would be sure to follow. Here's where my uncle and the sheikh lose me: If the black magic of laughter is so offensive, why isn't the hypnotic, lyrical effect of the Arabic language, recited aloud, also frowned upon?

Given that I glimpsed this silly side of Islam because of someone's expressed hope for a punch line involving a priest, a rabbi, and a mullah, I have to say that I love the curiosity of the public. For years, that curiosity has nourished my own. The more opportunities I've seized to be in the spotlight, getting noisy about this social problem or that global trend, the more I've needed outsiders to keep me on my toes about why I bother associating with a faith that beats at the center of so much international turmoil and individual torment. People are right to ask. Two questions, in particular, have rocked my world—both for the better, but neither without pain.

The first question is, "How do you reconcile homosexuality with Islam?" I'm openly lesbian. I choose to be "out" because, having matured in a miserable household under a father who despised joy, I'm not about to sabotage the consensual love that offers me joy as an adult. I met my first girlfriend in my twenties and, weeks afterwards, told my mother about the relationship. She responded like the wonderful parent she is. So the question of whether I could be a Muslim and a lesbian at the same time barely unsettled me. *That* was religion. *This* was happiness. I knew which one I needed more. I carried on, intermittently studying Islam, learning the fine art of sustaining relationships with women (which is another book unto itself), producing television programs, and generally living the multidirectional life of a twenty-something in North America.

As my TV work made me a more visible public figure, my hope of reconciling homosexuality with Islam evolved into a preoccupation. Viewers wanted me to justify my improbable combination of identities. I was plunged into a serious bout of introspection, even flirting with the possibility of finally giving up Islam for the sake of love. Hey, what better motive is there to sacrifice anything? But each time I reached the brink of excommunicating myself, I pulled back. Not out of fear. Out of fairness—to myself. One question begged for more thought: If the all-knowing, all-powerful God didn't wish to make me a lesbian, then why didn't He make someone else in my place?

Hostile challenges to "explain myself" became a near daily occurrence after 1998. That year, I started hosting *QueerTelevision,* an unprecedented TV and Internet series about gay and lesbian cultures. The show was about people, not porn, and yet avowed Muslims joined Christian fundamentalists in petitioning against my presence on their screens. In truth, I expected nothing less. But was I naive to expect a little more—conversation, instead of mere condemnation?

Believe me, I tried to do the dialogue thing. As a lover of diversity, including diversity of perspectives, I never trashed my detractors' missives. In fact, I regularly aired them on the program. An example: "I am writing to inform you that the one and only real God, the God of the Bible, makes it painfully clear that all Sodomites (meaning 'homosexuals' or like deviants) have forsaken their humanity for their deranged, perverted, evil lusts. Thereby they have become abominations, no longer human, and are to be executed immediately according to Leviticus and Deuteronomy . . ."

The many Muslims who called and e-mailed *QueerTelevision* agreed with these Christians. (Except for the part about the one and only real God belonging strictly to the Bible.) Yet not a single Muslim addressed my counterchallenge, my repeated stab at conversation: How can the Koran at once denounce homosexuality and declare that Allah "makes excellent everything He creates"? How do my critics explain the fact that, according to the book by which they scrupulously abide, God has deliberately designed the world's breathtaking multiplicity? The question that pits homosexuality against Islam tested my faith alright. But thinking it through has made me realize that a healthy exchange is possible if we all care less about where we stand than where God might.

Now for the second question I promised to tell you about. It was asked of me mere months before September 11, and it precipitated my biggest test of faith.

In December 2000, an interoffice envelope arrived on my desk at *QueerTelevision*. The envelope came from my boss, Moses Znaimer. Scrambling to complete as many episodes of the program as possible by Christmas break, I felt at once drained and in need of distraction. So I opened the envelope and pulled out a newspaper clipping. It featured a brief report from the *Agence France-Presse*:

GIRL COERCED INTO SEX TO RECEIVE 180 LASHES

Tsafe [Nigeria]. A pregnant 17-year-old whom an Islamic court sentenced to 180 lashes for premarital sex will give birth within days, her family said yesterday.

Bariya Ibrahim Magazu told the court in September that she had been pushed into having sex with three men who were associates of her father. The girl produced seven witnesses. The girl's family said she was due to give birth within a couple of days and was expected to receive her punishment at least 40 days later. AFP

In vibrant red ink, Moses had circled the word "Islamic," twice underlined the number "180," and penned a comment, Talmud-style, in the margins. It read:

IRSHAD
ONE OF THESE
DAYS YOU'LL
TELL ME HOW
YOU RECONCILE
THIS KIND OF
INSANITY,
AND FEMALE
GENITAL
MUTILATION,
WITH YOUR
MUSLIM
FAITH.
M.

Oy vey. Wasn't it enough that viewers of *QueerTelevision* goaded me to choose between my sexual orientation and my spiritual orientation? Did my boss have to burden me ethically, too? Especially at a time of excruciating deadlines?

I pushed the envelope aside and got on with working for the

man. But over the next several hours, Moses's challenge shook my conscience. Tell me it doesn't do the same to yours. The story of this young rape victim has to haunt any decent human being because, whatever the minutiae of her case, one reported fact couldn't be rationalized away: The woman, her dignity already violated, had gone to the trouble of rounding up seven witnesses. Seven! And she still faced 180 lashes! How the hell could I reconcile such an elemental injustice with my Muslim faith?

I was going to have to address it head-on. Not with defensiveness, not with theories, but with total honesty. Less than a year before much of the world was to be unmoored by September 11, I prepared to enter the next chapter of my life as a Muslim Refusenik.

2

SEVENTY VIRGINS?

Since becoming a madressa casualty, I'd grappled with the over-riding question: Should I bid good-bye to Islam? In order to answer that one, I had to tackle the question of whether there's something cardinal, something inextricably core, within Islam that makes it more rigid today than its spiritual siblings, Christianity and Judaism. My boss's challenge propelled me headfirst into the swamp.

What disturbed me wasn't just the story of one Nigerian rape victim. Pick a Muslim country, any Muslim country, and the most brutal humiliations will grab you by the vitals. In Pakistan, an average of two women every day die from "honor killings," often with Allah's name on the lips of the murderers. In Mali and Mauritania, little boys are seduced into slavery by Muslim hustlers. In Sudan, slavery happens at the hands of Islamic militias. In Yemen and Jordan, Christian humanitarian workers have been shot point-blank. In Bangladesh, artists who advocate for the rights of religious minorities have been locked up or driven out of the country altogether. It's all documented.

Ah yes, I'm confusing culture with religion again. But am I? Even in Toronto, whose culture differs markedly from that of Bangladesh, a cruel, crude brand of Islam thrives. Stick with me as I tell you how I know this.

Shortly after receiving Moses' envelope, I devoted an episode of *QueerTelevision* to the reality of gay and lesbian Muslims. The stories starred a gay man who'd left Pakistan to live in London, and a lesbian who'd fled her native Iran for Vancouver.

Miriam, the lesbian, had been branded "corrupt of the earth" by religious police in her homeland. I ran video footage smuggled from Iran to prove what would have happened to her if she'd stayed and been arrested. The tape showed two women, bundled alive in white sheets, being lowered into freshly dug pits. A mob of men and boys gathered around them and began to hurl fist-sized stones at their heads. Most hit the mark and bounced off to reveal crimson spurting from the material. Miriam explained that, by law, every rock-hurler was supposed to tuck a Koran under his arm to restrain the force of the throw. That decree didn't always stick. Still fearing for her life, Miriam told her story in silhouette.

Adnan, the gay Muslim man, agreed to appear on camera. He believed that the Koran rules against homosexuality, but he had made peace with this verdict. After all, Adnan didn't intend to bring his boyfriend home to all Muslims, just to his mother in Pakistan. Religious validation, while nice to have, wasn't necessary—not, at any rate, in liberated London, where he and his boyfriend lived. The episode ended with an advisor to London's Islamic Cultural Centre commenting on the need to be humble when judging gays and lesbians. Although it appears that Islam doesn't tolerate homosexuality, he said, "anything's possible" with a majestic God.

You know what happened after the show aired? Of all the complaints I got from Toronto-area Muslims, the most common was that these homosexual "pigs" and "dogs" whom I had featured must have been—brace yourself—Jews. Never mind the heinous video of Iranian stoning practices, or Adnan's willingness to accept a theological thumbs-down about his sexuality, or the religious advisor's call for God-conscious humility on everyone's part. None of it registered with the incensed Muslims who wrote and phoned in. Only one thing scanned—that gays and lesbians couldn't possibly be part of "us." Homosexuals are manifestly moles for "them." This, from the bosom of a twenty-first-century cosmopolis.

I was nauseated. Whatever the culture in which Muslims lived, be it rural or digital, and whatever the generation, whether symbolized by a 1970s mosque for immigrants or by a media-connected city for the new millennium, Islam emerged as desperately tribal. Did we ever need a reformation.

But what did that mean—a "reformation"? Truthfully, I had only the sketchiest idea. What I knew was that believers in the historically "reformed" religions don't operate on a herd mentality nearly as much as Muslims do. Christian leaders are aware of the intellectual diversity within their ranks. While each can deny the validity of other interpretations—and many do—none can deny that a plethora of interpretations exists. As for Jews, they're way ahead of the crowd. Jews actually publicize disagreements by surrounding their scriptures with commentaries and incorporating debates into the Talmud itself. By contrast, most Muslims treat the Koran as a document to imitate rather than interpret, suffocating our capacity to think for ourselves.

Even in the West, Muslims are routinely taught that the Koran is the final manifesto of God's will, displacing the Bible and the Torah. As the final manifesto, it's the "perfect" scripture—not to be questioned, analyzed, or even interpreted, but simply believed. Indeed, the first word that Prophet Muhammad heard from the Angel Gabriel, speaking on behalf of God, was "Recite!" Other translations have it as "Read!" Either way, mouthing the words in order to imitate them is as far as the majority of us ever go. Anything more would be, well, interpretation.

It's the same deal with a second source of Islamic theology, the *hadiths*. These are "authoritative" reports of what Prophet Muhammad said and did throughout his life. Whatever question the Koran doesn't readily answer—note the word, "readily"— the hadiths supposedly do. Over the centuries, they've been gathered and catalogued by scholars of the highest repute for our consumption. All we have to do is submit to them (or, more accurately, to the ones that our imams select for us). Oh, and about the minor problem that Prophet Muhammad was eminently human and vulnerable to honest errors of judgment? Hush. Since the hadiths reflect the life of God's last messenger to humanity, doubting them can't be tolerated.

Do you see where this express train of goodness is actually taking us? To a destination called Brain-Dead. When abuse occurs under the aegis of Islam, a minority of Muslims know how to argue, reassess, or reform. Which is just as well, we're told, since abuse can't occur as long as we stay true to the perfect text. Aaargh! What asylum logic! Such circular conditioning of the mind is enough to turn the brightest bulbs into dimwits, and dangerous ones at that.

Of course, every faith has adherents who ape. The difference is, only in contemporary Islam is imitation *mainstream*.

Bruce Feiler is an American writer who tapped into that difference while researching his book *Abraham: A Journey into the Heart of Three Faiths.* In Jerusalem, Feiler met with the imam of Al-Aksa Mosque, Sheikh Abu Sneina. The imam stressed Islam's presumed perfection. In London-honed English, he told Feiler that "You must follow the last prophet" whom God has sent. Otherwise, "You'll die" under God's blowtorch, just as millions of Jews had been "grilled alive" with divine sanction by Hitler. Feiler left the interview disgusted, and later related the incident to a journalist specializing in religion. "The unfortunate truth," said the journalist, "is that [Sheikh Sneina] represents the mainstream in Islam at the moment. You can find Jews who have a similar message of Jewish nationalism, but not that many. You can find apocalyptic Christians, but still a limited number. Your imam represents the bulk of Muslims, at least around here."

Sneina exemplifies the mind-set of many a Muslim, not just in Jerusalem but also in the diaspora. Let me quote from a 2002 report put out by the Academy for Learning Islam, based in my hometown of Richmond. The academy claims that Islam's two major sects, the Sunnis and the Shias, have much in common. How so? "Both believe in the absolute veracity and perfection of the Holy Qur'an. Both consider Muhammad as the last Messenger of God and struggle to imitate his sayings and practices." When imitation goes mainstream, most of us fail to explore our prejudices—or even acknowledge that we have any. We believe what we're supposed to believe, and that's that.

The disapproving mail I would get as host of *QueerTelevision* illustrates what I mean. Any time I aired antigay comments from Bible-citing Christians, other Christians would be sure to follow up with rival, tolerant interpretations. That never happened when

Muslims bawled me out. Apparently, there was no question that they spoke for Islam. All of it. Which is not to say that every last Muslim objects to homosexuals. Al-Fatiha, a queer Muslim group, has chapters in big cities across North America and Europe. In Toronto, at least, its annual dinner is attracting the attendance of some Muslim parents. But even if many Muslims don't share the prejudices of mainstream Islam, neither do enough of us create conversations with the mainstream. How else to explain why not one Muslim wrote or called *QueerTelevision* with an alternate—compassionate—interpretation of the Koran?

Against this backdrop, I felt ready not only to confront Moses' challenge, but to expand on it. To start figuring out whether Islam was irredeemably rigid, I had to take on the question of "others" in Islam—women, yes, but also Jews. And Christians. And slaves. And anybody else whose plight epitomizes the suffusive brutality in the Muslim world today. What does the Koran say about these creatures of God? Does it unequivocally, or even plausibly, support whipping a raped woman despite a multitude of witnesses to the crime against her? While we're at it, does the Koran really prohibit women from leading prayer?

For the next few months, I reread Islam's holy book with eyes open wider and defenses further down than at any other point in my life.

IN THE BEGINNING, THERE WAS THE WOMAN QUESTION. WHOM did God create first—Adam or Eve? The Koran is dead silent on this distinction. God breathed life into a "single soul," and from that soul he "created its spouse." Who's the soul and who's the spouse? It's irrelevant.

Moreover, there's no mention of Adam's rib, from which,

according to the Bible, Eve was made. Nor does the Koran suggest that Eve tempted Adam to taste forbidden fruit. Bottom line: You can't find fodder here for male superiority. Just the opposite, in fact. The Koran cautions Muslims to remember that they're not God, so men and women had better be fair in demanding their rights from one another. And topping off this passage is a seemingly female-friendly flourish: "Honor the mothers who bore you. God is ever watching over you."

Strange thing is, in the same chapter—mere lines away—the Koran completely reverses course. It says: "Men have authority over women because God has made the one superior to the other, and because they spend their wealth to maintain them. Good women are obedient. . . . As for those from whom you fear disobedience, admonish them, forsake them in beds apart, and beat them."

Let me get this straight: To deserve a beating, a woman doesn't actually have to disobey anybody, a man merely has to fear her disobedience. His insecurity becomes her problem. Swell. I know I'm oversimplifying, but oversimplification runs rampant in the development of god-awful laws. I'll give you a concrete example. One line from the Koran—that men can lord it over women because they "spend their wealth to maintain" them—has influenced the Cairo Declaration, the specious human rights charter endorsed by Muslim countries in 1990. Sure, one clause of the charter affirms that women and men enjoy equal dignity. But the next clause designates men as the providers of their families. It's not expressing a *preference* for men as providers, it's making an outright proclamation that "the husband is responsible for the support and welfare of the family." And since the Koran states that husbands can claim "authority over women" through the role of providing, you figure out the rest.

In light of the raped woman in Nigeria, one more passage from the Koran bowled me over. "Women are your fields," it says. "Go, then, into your fields when you please. Do good works and fear God." Huh? Go into women when you please, yet do good? Are women partners or property? Partners, insists Jamal Badawi, a renowned Koranic scholar. He assures me that this "sexually enlightened" verse serves as a defense of foreplay. Like fields, women need tender loving care in order to turn sperm into real human beings. The farmer's "seed is worthless unless you have the fertile land that will give it growth," Badawi says, looking quite satisfied with his progressive explanation. But he has only addressed the words, "Go into your fields." What about the words, "when you please"? Doesn't that qualifier give men undue power? The question remains: Which paradigm does Allah advocate—Adam and Eve as equals, or women as land to be plowed (excuse me, stroked) on a whim?

The truth is, I knew which interpretation I wanted but I didn't know for sure (and still don't) which one God wanted. With so much contradiction at play, nobody knows. Those who wish to flog women on the flimsiest of charges can get the necessary backup from the Koran. So can those who don't want girls to lead prayer. Then again, those who seek equality can find succor, too.

In trying to answer how I reconcile my Muslim faith with the barbaric lashing of a rape victim, I concluded that I couldn't reconcile them with breezy confidence. I couldn't glibly say, as I've heard so many Muslim feminists do, that the Koran itself guarantees justice. I couldn't cavalierly shrug that those whacko Nigerian jurists who apply Sharia law have sodomized my transparently egalitarian religion. The Koran is not transparently egalitarian for women. It's not transparently anything except enigmatic. With apologies to Noam Chomsky, it's Muslims who manufacture consent in Allah's name. The decisions we make on the basis of the Koran aren't dictated by God; we make them of our free human will.

Sounds obvious to a mainstream Christian or Jew, but it's not obvious to a Muslim who's been raised to believe—as most of us have—that the Koran lays it all out for us in a "straight path," and that our sole duty, and right, is to imitate it. This is a big lie. Do you hear me? A big, beard-faced lie.

Far from being perfect, the Koran is so profoundly at war with itself that Muslims who "live by the book" have no choice but to choose what to emphasize and what to downplay. Maybe that's the easy part—any one of us can rationalize our biases by elevating one verse and ignoring another. Which, by the way, liberals do as much as militants, airbrushing the negative noise of the Koran at least as much as our opponents expunge its positive pronouncements. We all have agendas, some more equal than others.

But as long as we're caught up in this endgame of proving that "our" dogma trumps "their" dogma, we're losing sight of the greater challenge. That is, to openly question the perfection of the Koran so that the stampede to reach a correct conclusion about what it "really" says will slow down and, over time, become an exercise in literacy instead of literalism. At this stage, reform isn't about telling ordinary Muslims what not to think, but about giving Islam's 1 billion devotees permission to think. Since the Koran is a bundle of contradictions, at least when it comes to women, we have every reason to think.

To push this idea further, I had to see whether there's a pattern to the Koran's blatant inconsistencies. Put simply, is Islam's scripture also vague or conflicted about other human rights issues, such as slavery? If so, do twenty-first-century Muslims have the room to make twenty-first-century choices? I thought of Sudan and later read about the extent of its slave trade. In Khartoum, "a Taliban-like Muslim regime is waging a self-declared jihad" on Christians, animists, and non-Arab Muslims. That's according to Charles Jacobs, president of the American Anti-Slavery Group and director of the Sudan Campaign. Jacobs observes that "Khartoum's onslaught has rekindled the trade in black slaves, halted (mostly) a century ago by the British abolitionists. . . . [A]fter the men are slaughtered, the women, girls, and boys are gangraped—or they have their throats slit for resisting. The terrorized survivors are marched northward and distributed to Arab masters, the women to become concubines, the girls domestics, the boys goatherders."

I thought once more of northern Nigeria, another place where Islamic governments encourage the enslavement of Christians. Okay, I accept that Nigeria's civil war has more to do with politics than religion. Still, all these primitive forms of politics couldn't be waged without some help from the Koran. How much help—that was my question. I went to the source and discovered this passage: "As for those of your slaves who wish to buy their liberty, free them if you find in them any promise . . ."

Whoa. I had to pause and parse that one. Read it closely and you'll find that the Koran doesn't direct us to release all slaves, just those who their owners decide have the potential to achieve a better standing. How's that for appealing to our subjective sensibilities, to our ethical agency, to our freedom of choice? In other words, Muslims today can maneuver their way out of the seventh century with the Koran's consent—if we opt to. The Koran grants Nigerian legislators the choice to update, which is to say eliminate, the scourge of slavery. As with women, so with slaves:

The decisions that Muslims make are ours alone. They can't be laid at God's feet.

Could it be that Islam doesn't merely tolerate individual Muslims interpreting the Koran for themselves, but that such engagement and exploration might even be the *only* way to "Know Your Islam"?

Energized, I moved to another huge human rights file: the treatment of non-Muslims. Because Islam comes from Judeo-Christian traditions, the Koran has a lot to say about Jews and Christians. It heaps affection on Abraham, grandfather of the three monotheisms. It extols Jesus as "Messiah" more than once. Christ's mother, Mary, gets several positive mentions. To boot, the Koran reminds us of the Jews' "exalted" nationhood! Exalted? The Jews? I checked a few English translations just to be sure. Given all these warm fuzzies for our spiritual forebears, it makes sense that the Koran would advise Jews and Christians to relax, that they have "nothing to fear or regret" as long as they remain loyal to their scriptures.

On the other hand, the Koran explicitly anoints Islam as the only "true faith." Weird. Or is it? There's an ultra-important idea here—it couldn't be more important for our divided times—and it relates to why Islam came into being at all.

Everything Muslims ought to believe was revealed thousands of years before us to the Jews. It was when some Jews strayed from the revealed Truth, by worshiping idols such as the golden calf, that they incurred God's wrath. (I know, I know: What kind of Creator envies a baby cow? I'd say a Creator that's striving to bring together incessantly warring tribes through the focal point of a shared faith.) Back to the cow. The resurgence of idolatry necessitated that another child of Abraham be sent to remind the Semitic world of its Lord's Truth. Thus the arrival of Jesus.

Thus, too, the Bible, which incorporates the Hebrew Books of Moses (known to Christians as the Old Testament). Eventually, though, certain Christians began claiming that Jesus was God as well as the son of God rather than a human emissary chosen by the one and only God. Idolatry threatened to rear its head (or heads!) yet again.

So, around 610 C.E., God revisited the prophet pool and selected Muhammad, another descendent of Abraham, to tidy the mess that both the Jews and the Christians had made of His revelations. That's why Islam returns to original Jewish teachings for its inspiration and integrity. No matter where I opened the Koran, I was never far from an oft-repeated message, namely, that earlier scriptures deserve reverence.

Welcome to the ultra-important idea that I alluded to moments ago: Tribal arrogance can't be Truth. As I reread the Koran for insights into the "other," I came to see that it's not *all* Jews whom Muslims are told to avoid but those Jews who mock Islam as inherently false. And Muslims shouldn't deny the validity of Judaism; otherwise, we're discrediting our own faith.

But if Judaism and Islam are a single faith, what's the point of having them as separate entities? For that matter, what's the point of retaining Christianity? Or Hinduism, Buddhism, Sikhism, fill-in-the-blankism? Why can't we lose all the sacramental one-upmanship and view each other as the handiwork of a common Creator? The Koran doesn't shy away from that most vexing of questions. Different religions ought to exist, it says, so that human beings feel an incentive to compete in "good works." It admits that good can't be done by entangling ourselves in disputes over who's "truly" implementing God's will. You and I can't know, so we've got to cut through that clutter. The Koran assures us that God will settle our doctrinal spats once we return to Him. In the meantime, competing in good works is an entrepreneurial-cum-artistic call to take the same hunk of scriptural clay and continually improve on the beauty of the product. Endemic to that exercise is God's other motive for creating various peoples: so we'll feel an incentive to know one another. It's as if the Creator intended us to use difference as an icebreaker rather than as an excuse to retreat into opposite corners.

Admittedly, that's what I'd like it all to mean. But everything's up for interpretation, because the Koran also discourages Muslims from taking Jews and Christians as friends, lest we become "one of them." It speaks of "them" as an "unjust people" whom "God does not guide." There's talk of smiting, slaughtering, and subjecting non-Muslims to a special tax as a tribute to their Muslim conquerors. Truly scalding stuff, these passages lend credence to those Muslims who spit on interfaith outreach. For such people, non-Muslims can exist, but never on a level playing field with Muslims. Not anywhere close to level, because Islam isn't one faith in addition to the rest, it supersedes the rest by dint of having the perfect word and the final prophet in service to the one God. It's a choice to read the Koran this way, isn't it? But we're not conscious that we're choosing it.

"Slow down," you might protest. "I'm not choosing this interpretation at all. I don't want to smack my neighbor for celebrating Hanukkah, so don't lump me in with the Jew-bashers. I'm decent, dammit." Yes, you probably are. Out of decency, then, ask yourself this: Have I chosen to challenge the mainstream Muslim belief that Islam trumps Christianity and Judaism? So thoroughly immersed are we in our spiritual narcissism that most Muslims don't think twice, or once, about the damage this attitude can inflict on the world. We instinctively accept it, sliding our heads out of the sand every so often to notice the "extremists." And sometimes not even then.

Do I exaggerate? Tell me after you read this story. A few weeks before September 11, I joined a panel of Muslims on national TV to "discuss images of the Islamic world." Taking this politely worded invitation as a euphemism for "let's complain about the West," my fellow panelists indulged in the usual casti-gating of North American pop culture: Hollywood casts us all as fanatics, the fanatics always look swarthy, and every other stan-dard line in the victims' canon. Bored with an argument-on-autopilot, I proposed a different line: that we Muslims don't give people much incentive to see us as anything but monolithic. Where, I asked, were Muslims in Toronto, Vancouver, or Mon-treal when the Taliban toppled the pre-Islamic statues of Bud-dha that overlooked Afghanistan's Bamiyan Valley? "Let there be no compulsion in religion," says the Koran. We couldn't expect the Taliban to sing that tune, but why didn't Muslims in the West choose to sing it rather than remain mostly mute? Why the absence of mass Muslim protests in our own streets?

I waited.

The sole response came from another Muslim woman—an active feminist, no less. "Manji," she blurted, "do you know what's happening to Muslims in Palestine?" Excuse me?! Some-body return me to earth, or transport my butt to a part of the solar system where we distinguish between justice and justifica-tion. I'll give her this much: There's obviously some relationship between the rise of Islamic totalitarianism and the intractable politics of the Middle East. But how did that textured relation-ship justify Muslim silence in the West toward the scripturally supremacist, Buddha-bombing, woman-pulverizing, kite-banning, execution-enamored Taliban?

It didn't. The response of my "sister" was a cop-out. For all her critical thinking about the West, she wore her unthinking Islam like a head-to-toe burqa. If that was the best a self-proclaimed feminist could do, I shuddered to imagine where we were all headed.

EVERYBODY FOCUSES ON THE DATE OF SEPTEMBER 11. I WANT TO focus on the days following. What did we Muslims assure the media, politicians, and ourselves about Islam? With morose faces, we said that our faith had been "hijacked." That's right, America, hijacked. We're one with you, Germany. We love our freedom, too, Australia. We're in this together, Canada. We, along with you, have been hijacked.

I couldn't stand this metaphor. It implied that Islam itself was a plane cruising toward some haven of human rights, and that, had September 11 not happened, the passengers of Air Koranistan would have reached their wondrous address with nary a bump, thank you very much. Hijacked. As if our religion were an innocent bystander in the violence perpetrated by Muslims. Hijacked. An emotionally charged word that acquits mainstream Muslims of the responsibility to be self-critical. First and foremost, being self-critical means coming clean about the nasty side of the Koran, and how it informs terrorism.

Post–September 11, I repeatedly heard this mantra from Muslims: The Koran makes it absolutely clear when jihad can and can't be pursued, and the terrorists unquestionably broke the rules. To quote one such voice, Allah "says in unequivocal terms that to kill an innocent being is like killing entire humanity." Wishful whitewashing, I say. You know the chapter and verse that's cited as "unequivocal"? It actually bestows wiggle room.

Here's how it reads: "We laid it down for the Israelites that who-ever killed a human being, except as punishment for murder or other villainy in the land, shall be regarded as having killed all mankind." Sadly, the clause starting with "except" can be deployed by militant Muslims to fuel their jihads.

Osama bin Laden, for example, announced a jihad against the entire United States in the late 1990s. The Koran helped him. Go back to the phrase, "except as punishment for murder or other villainy in the land." Did economic sanctions against Iraq, imposed by the UN but demanded by Washington, cause the "murder" of half a million children and counting? Bin Laden believes so. Would the bootprints of American troops in Saudi soil qualify as "villainy in the land"? To bin Laden, you bet. As for American civilians, can they be innocent of either "murder" or "villainy" when their tax money helps Israel buy tanks to raze Palestinian homes? A no-brainer for bin Laden. As he told CNN in 1997, "The U.S. government has committed acts that are extremely unjust, hideous, and criminal, through its sup-port of the Israeli occupation of Palestine. Due to its subordi-nation to the Jews, the arrogance of the United States has reached the point that they've occupied Arabia, the holiest place of the Muslims. For this and other acts of aggression and injustice, we have declared jihad against the United States."

You and I can agree that Osama bin Laden is morally Nean-derthal for pursuing this strain of jihad. But can we agree that he and his mercenaries have been scripturally supported too? All I'm asking for is honesty.

What's that? I should understand the context of the Koran's violent passages? Let me assure you: I've read the scholarship that explains these verses "in their context," and I think there's a fancy dance of evasion going on. It's not choreographed by conspiracy, just by a deep-seated assumption that the Koran is perfect, so there must be perfectly valid reasons for the hate it often preaches.

Consider one high-profile argument that defends "authentic" Islam as a religion of peace. According to this argument, since God advised Prophet Muhammad in good times and bad, the Koran's bad verses merely reflect the bad times Muhammad faced in his twenty-five or so years of spreading Islam. Muhammad began by proselytizing in Mecca, where slaves, widows, orphans, and the working poor latched onto his unconventional message of mercy. God knows, these outcasts needed a dose of mercy in the economically stratified and morally decadent money capital of Arabia. At first, then, the Koran's revelations emphasized compassion.

But within no time the business establishment of Mecca grew threatened—and threatening. Muhammad and his flock pulled up stakes and moved to Medina in order to protect themselves. Basically, that's when the Koran's message of compassion turns to retribution. In Medina, some residents welcomed the Muslim influx and others decidedly didn't. Among those who didn't were Medina's prominent Jewish tribes, who colluded with Mecca's pagans to assassinate Muhammad and annihilate Islam's converts. The reason they failed is that God instructed Muhammad to strike preemptively. According to the argument, this is where all the vitriol in the Koran comes from. However, continues the argument, retribution isn't the spirit with which Muslims started out. They resorted to it for the purpose of self-preservation, and only temporarily. The older, "authentic," message of Islam is the one on which Muhammad launched his religion. It's the message of justice, equality, unity—peace.

How emotionally comforting. While I would have loved to

believe this account of things, the more I read and reflected, the less sense it made. For starters, it's not clear which verses came to Muhammad when. The Koran appears to be organized by size of verse—from longer to shorter—and not by chronology of revelation. How can anyone isolate the "earlier" passages, let alone read into them the "authentic" message of the Koran? We have to own up to the fact that the Koran's message is all over the bloody map. Compassion and contempt exist side by side. Look at its take on women. Hopeful and hateful verses stand only lines away from each other. So, too, with religious diversity. There's no single thrust in this so-called perfect, indisputable, and straightforward text. The Koran's perfection is, ultimately, suspect.

Oh dear. Have I crossed the line? My own line-crossing pales compared to that of the Al-Qaeda terrorists. Unlike me, these guys set out to murder. If we're sincere about fighting the asphyx-iating despotism they represent, we can't be afraid to ask: What if the Koran isn't perfect? What if it's not a completely God-authored book? What if it's riddled with human biases?

Let's take up that possibility for a minute. Mohamed Atta, leader of the September 11 kamikazes, wrote a homicide note on behalf of his gang. In the note, he said, "It is enough for us that [the Koran's verses] are the words of the Creator of the Earth and the planets . . ." Not once, but three times, Atta referred to taking solace in "all the things that God has promised the martyrs." In particular, "Know that the gardens of paradise are waiting for you in all their beauty, and the women of para-dise are waiting, calling out, 'Come hither, friend of God.' "

Allow me to decode this B-movie lingo for you: Atta and the boys expected unfettered access to dozens of virgins in heaven. They're not the only ones. A month before September 11, a recruiter for the Palestinian resistance-turned-terror outfit Hamas told CBS television that he dangles the vision of seventy virgins in front of candidates. It's like a perpetual license to ejaculate in exchange for a willingness to detonate, and it's long been claimed that the Koran promises this reward to Muslim martyrs.

But we have reason to believe that there's trouble in paradise, a human error that's made its way into the Koran. According to new research, what martyrs can anticipate for their sacrifices aren't virgins but raisins! The word that Koranic scholars have for centuries read as "dark-eyed virgins"—*hur*—might be more accurately understood as "white raisins." (Don't laugh. Not excessively, anyway. Raisins would have been pricey enough delicacies in seventh-century Arabia to be considered a heavenly treat.) Still, raisins instead of virgins? Please. How can the Koran be so mistaken?

The historian who makes this case, Christoph Luxemberg, is a specialist in Middle Eastern languages. He traces the Koran's description of heaven to a Christian work written three centuries before Islam in a form of Aramaic, the language Jesus likely spoke. If the Koran drew influences from Judeo-Christian culture—which would be entirely in keeping with its claim of reflecting earlier revelations—then Aramaic would have been translated by human hand into Arabic. Or *mis*translated in the case of *hur* and who knows how many other words.

What if entire phrases have been misconceived? As an illiterate trader, Prophet Muhammad relied on scribes to jot down the words he heard from God. Sometimes the Prophet himself had an agonizing go at deciphering what he heard. That's how a set of "satanic verses"—passages that deified heathen idols—reportedly passed muster with Muhammad and got recorded as authentic entries for the Koran. The Prophet later dropped those verses, blaming them on a trick played by Satan. Yet, the fact that Muslim philosophers throughout the centuries have told this story speaks to age-old doubts about the Koran's perfection. Now more than ever, we need to bring back the doubts.

What if Mohamed Atta had been raised on soul-stretching questions instead of simple certitudes? At the very least, what if this college student had known that the origins of select words—pivotal words about the hereafter—can be contested? That they might not all be the "words of the Creator of the Earth and the planets"? That the payoff for self-immolation, to say nothing of mass murder, is dubious? That the prospect of paradise is guesswork, not a guarantee? Maybe then he would have stepped back. Maybe. The possibility begs for attention.

The very act of questioning the Koran is a central piece of the reform puzzle because it signals a breach with the herd. It means you're not going to accept that the answers are a given, or that they're going to be given to you.

In the months after September 11, one question above all others pestered me: Since the Koran makes room for the exercise of free will, why do the governing geniuses of Islam seem to default into narrowness? Why don't more of them choose the path of openness? I had to go beyond the Koran. I had to find the incubator of Pavlovian Muslim prejudices.

To do so, I had to peel back more layers on the lies we're telling.

3

WHEN DID WE
STOP THINKING?

By November 2001, we'd all had nearly two months to absorb the looped images. Profiles of the World Trade Center dead played endlessly on our TVs, a memorial as much to the unshakeable as to the unthinkable. But public numbness did wane, as it must, and the how-could-it-happen interviews took on a sharper tone. One question would no longer be put off: What did Islam have to do with this assault?

Right out of the gate, Islamic organizations in North America had dispatched a steady stream of conciliatory press releases. The bylines of their leaders showed up in newspaper opinion pages. Day in, day out on cable news, "race relations" lobbyists implored Americans and their allies not to vent their frustrations on Muslims, because the overwhelming majority of us are "the good guys." Friends in Europe sent me examples of similar platitudes being bandied around in their media.

Muslim mouthpieces practically exclaimed, Hey BBC, we've agreed to be on your airwaves, we're confessing that something's askew within Islam. What more do you want? Look, Reuters, we're out there slamming the militants. Go ahead, quote us! Yo, Fox, we're debating your conservative pals, not ducking them, so don't accuse us of covering our asses.

Then *I'll* accuse us of covering our asses. For all our denunciations of Islam's fringe sickness, Muslims studiously avoided addressing the paralyzing sickliness of the entire religion—the untouchability of mainstream Islam.

Two months after September 11, I did what I knew I could. I wrote a series of articles calling for introspection. After all, Muslims who live in the West have the luxury of posing hard questions without fear of state reprisal. The twin towers that didn't deserve to collapse lay in rubble; the twin towers that did deserve to collapse continued to prop up a palatable yet unexamined version of Islam. Tower one: a deceit. Tower two: a conceit.

The deceit, I explained, was that instead of acknowledging a serious problem with the practice of this religion today, we reflexively romanticized Islam. The peer pressure to stay on message—the message being that *we're not all terrorists*—seduced us into avoiding the most crucial of jihads: self-criticism. Enough of this adolescent capitulation to peer pressure. Enough, too, of wallowing in the conceit that Westerners owe us basic human respect, but we owe nothing to the Western values that offer us this opportunity for respect. In one of my articles, I pointed out that after September 11, a Toronto-based Muslim group urged politicians to speak out against anti-Muslim bigotry. Among those who did was an openly gay politician. I wrote that I hoped he could expect reciprocal outrage from Muslims the next time a gay club or bookstore got firebombed.

I summarized my challenge to fellow Muslims this way: Will

we remain spiritually infantile, shackled by expectations to clam up and conform, or will we mature into full-fledged citizens, defending the very pluralism of interpretations and ideas that makes it possible for us to observe Islam in this part of the world?

Responses flooded in. Non-Muslims craved more candor. So did a few Muslims. Most Muslims, however, would have none of it. Some dismissed me as a traumatized madressa misfit, and they might have had a point about my personal condition. But as long as they insisted on talking trauma, why didn't I hear a peep from them about the wider trauma that a few faithful Muslims had wrought on September 11? What did they have to say about our religion's role in that devastation? Nothing. Others accused me of lashing out because I'd been rejected by the mainstream of Islam. Indeed, I had been rejected, and I'm not ashamed of that. Why would I aspire to be part of an intellectually atrophied and morally impaired mainstream?

I didn't argue with every letter, though. One correspondent in particular shut me up and compelled me to contemplate. Dismayed by the "harrowing picture" of Islam that I'd painted, this Muslim taught me something constructive. Did I know about *ijtihad?* he asked. Not j-i-h-a-d, but i-j-t-i-h-a-d. (He even helped me pronounce it: "IJ-tee-had.") Ijtihad, he told me, was the Islamic tradition of independent reasoning, which he claimed allowed every Muslim, female or male, straight or gay, old or young, to update his or her religious practice in light of contemporary circumstances.

Ij-tee-had. It's a tradition within Islam? It's about independent thought? I'll be damned. (Maybe literally.)

Reflecting on it further, I recalled coming across the word ijtihad in my post-madressa readings. But it had appeared without fanfare, presented more as a parched legalism than as a revolutionary concept. Besides, the impression I carried was that only religious authorities could legitimately engage in interpreting the Koran. Learning about ijtihad spurred me to ask: Who are these religious authorities? I mean, does the Koran recognize a formal clergy? Nope. Do the Koran's wild mood swings make any interpretation of its text selective and subjective? Yep. So, could it be that the right of independent thinking, the tradition of ijtihad, is in fact open to all of us? That by arrogating this right to themselves, the follow-my-fatwa ayatollahs are the actual heretics?

AS USUAL, I STARTED TO READ, SURF, AND TALK TO SCHOLARS. WHO made ijtihad a tradition? Where was it practiced and what did that society look like? I unearthed this portrait: The spirit of inquiry animated Islam's golden age, between about 750 and 1250 C.E. In Iraq, the heart of the Islamic empire, Christians worked alongside Muslims to translate and revive Greek philosophy. In Spain, the western rim of Islam's reach, Muslims developed what one Yale historian calls a "culture of tolerance" with Jews. Together, all of these communities gave us the precursor to globalization—the interconnectedness of technology, money, and people. Muslims traded vigorously with non-Muslims, pioneering a system by which checks could be prepared in Morocco and cashed in Syria. The back-and-forth of commerce cultivated a hopping traffic in ideas as well. Let me highlight a handful of Islam's contributions to Western culture. The guitar. Cough syrup. The university. Algebra. Mocha coffee. And the expression "Olé!," which has its root in "Allah!" (Blame the maracas on someone else.)

Innovation and the spirit of ijtihad went hand in glove. In the southern Spanish city of Cordoba, for example, a sexually spunky woman named Wallada organized literary salons where people analyzed dreams, poetry, and the Koran. They debated what the Koran proscribed for men and women. But what is a man? And what is a woman? They debated those questions too. The bounty and diversity of Koranic interpretations made this a time in which one could even discuss Islam's implications for hermaphrodites, people born with the genitals of both sexes.

Meanwhile, back in Baghdad, the center of empire bustled. Here sat Islam's *caliph*. Whether by election, slaughter, or a combination of both, the caliphs succeeded Prophet Muhammad as the leading statesmen and spiritual guides of the growing Muslim flock. It was in Baghdad that a ninth-century caliph, al-Mamun, constructed the so-called House of Wisdom—the "first institution of higher learning in the Islamic and Western world," according to Temple Univerisity's Mahmoud Ayoub. But competitive Cordoba wouldn't be outdone as a crucible of ideas; it became home to seventy libraries. That's one for every virgin today's Muslim martyrs believe they're pledged. Libraries then, virgins now—a telling contrast in priorities, wouldn't you say?

How did any of this foster an openness toward Jews and Christians? It's layered, but at rock bottom, tolerance served as the best way to build and maintain the Islamic empire. To begin with, most Muslim conquerors operated by the ground rule that you can't force conversion on fellow People of the Book—Jews and Christians. That rule proved to be imperialist Islam's strategic advantage over imperialist Christianity. Let's face it, crusading Catholics wouldn't have let Jews and heretic Christians practice their own faith. Muslims did, which ensured that they'd meet next to no resistance from religious minorities during wars to usurp territory. So, for example, Jews rejoiced when Muslims invaded Jerusalem in the year 638 C.E. and snatched the City of David away from the Byzantines, who had desecrated sacred Jew- ish sites by using them as garbage dumps. The victorious Muslims cleaned up the place and invited Jewish families to return.

Later, Jews kicked cooperation up one more notch and got in on the military action with Muslims. Suffering under zealously Catholic masters, the Jews of Spain begged the Muslims of Morocco to liberate them by taking over the Iberian Peninsula. A bizarre alliance developed: Muslims made Jews their lookouts against surprise advances from the pope's army. With intelli- gence gathered from Jews, Muslims sacked Spain in 711 C.E. (Along the way, their commander, Tarik bin Ziyad, crossed a hunk of rock whose current name, Gibraltar, hails from the Ara- bic for "Tarik's Mountain." It would be the first of many *Olé!* moments.)

The tricky part of empire isn't amassing it, but making it hum. That went double for the Arabs who, in the words of one culture critic, were "warriors, not administrators." But the war- riors had enough smarts to understand that they required a morning-after plan. So Muslim governors appointed the brightest of their subjects to run the swelling operations of empire. They needed deputies sensitive to the strains and sub- tleties of managing dislocated communities. They needed the global citizens of their era. Enter the Jews, and in grand fashion. From Spain to Iraq, Jews served as high-ranking diplomats, mil- itary lieutenants, court physicians, bankers, you name it.

I have to wonder if the Jews helped make Baghdad a natural choice for the capital of the Islamic empire. That's where, after the fall of the last Israelite kingdom in 70 C.E., the Jewish dias- pora set up a world-famous center for talmudic learning. When

Muslims arrived in Baghdad, this ancient Babylonian city already had an educated Jewish elite who could be tapped as a brain trust by the caliph. Which, in turn, smoothed the way for Baghdad's rabbis to transmit their teachings openly to Jews worldwide, 90 percent of whom lived under Muslim rulers. (In the ninth and tenth centuries, Jews made up half the population in parts of Spain.) Thanks to the easy flow of ideas at this time, says one scholar, "the Talmud and its interpretation of the Torah became the central authority in Jewish life."

You've got to love the symbiosis: As Islam hit its golden age, lifting influences from Jewish intellectual life, Jews made their own glorious strides, drawing inspiration from Arab Muslim culture. Secular Hebrew poetry poured from the pen of Shmuel ha-Nagid, the rabbi and amateur bard who served as prime minister in the Spanish courts of two Muslim monarchs. Take your time digesting that one.

None of this implies that Islamic civilization was all hand-holding harmony for Jews and Muslims. God no. From the eleventh century on, successive political regimes in Spain eroded tolerance with their tyranny. But even then, cultural convergence didn't immediately die out. Observers of all three Abrahamic faiths ran for their lives, resettled, and continued to marry each other, fusing everything from languages to fairy tales to philosophies.

I'll tell you whose career demonstrates the dynamism I'm talking about: Moses ben Maimon, or Maimonides, a top-tier Jewish philosopher, rabbi, physician, and ethicist. He published almost exclusively in Arabic. (Israel's first prime minister, David Ben-Gurion, learned Arabic during his lunch breaks so he could truly appreciate Maimonides.) And yet, Maimonides was no spiritual sellout. Besides being the first person to codify scriptural laws for the average Jew (the *Mishnah Torah,* which he wrote in Hebrew), the good doctor also authored the Jewish classic *The Guide for the Perplexed.* Recognizing that a frenzy of innovative thought can trigger moral confusion, Maimonides wanted Jews to retain sound scriptural principles without dumbing themselves down. This snippet from *The Guide for the Perplexed* demonstrates his intellectual honesty: "[I]t is in the nature of man to like what he is familiar with and in which he has been brought up, and that he fears anything alien. The plurality of religions and their mutual intolerance result from the fact that people remain faithful to the education they received."

What makes his career that much more admirable is that Maimonides lived in the precarious time after Muslim rowdies seized control of Cordoba, his birthplace. Around 1150 C.E., Maimonides and his family fled to North Africa, then to present-day Israel, before winding up in Egypt. There, he became physician to the top brass of Saladin, the Muslim military hero who frustrated the early wave of papal Crusaders. Given the not-so-distant drumbeat of Islamic extremism—in Spain if nowhere else—Maimonides could have withdrawn into his own religious or cultural absolutes. He didn't. In Egypt, he kept doctors' hours, and then some. He tended to the patients lining up at his door, studied with his Jewish community, and wrote for the wider world. Such was the unstoppable creative instinct of those who made the golden age glitter, even in its twilight.

Maimonides had a Muslim equal only nine years older than he—the philosopher, physician, mathematician, and fellow Cordoba native Ibn Rushd (often known by his Latin name, Averroes). Inside Spain, Ibn Rushd championed the very freedom to reason that Maimonides epitomized further east, daring to differ with the theocrats. Prompted by the rise of a ferocious Islam in his midst, Ibn Rushd argued that "philosophers are best able to understand properly the allegorical passages in the Koran on the basis of their logical training. There is no religious stipulation that all such passages have to be interpreted literally." Amen to that.

And why stop there? More than any other European of the time, Muslim or otherwise, Ibn Rushd spoke up for equality between the sexes. In his judgment, "the ability of women is not known" because they're "relegated to the business of procreation, child-rearing, and breast-feeding." He presciently warned the custodians of civilization that treating women like "a burden to the men" is "one of the reasons for poverty." With audacity like that, Ibn Rushd became a "burden" to the hyper-Muslim powers-that-be. They exiled him to Marrakech, Morocco, and on the eve of the thirteenth century, Ibn Rushd died under suspicious circumstances.

AS I MEDITATED ON WHAT MIGHT HAVE BEEN INFLICTED ON THE sparkling mind of Ibn Rushd, I kept asking, How could this happen? How could a haven of heterodoxy such as Muslim Spain become an outpost of orthodoxy? When did the rest of the Muslim empire stop thinking? What sealed the end of Islam's golden age, and what does it mean for all of us today?

First things first: It turns out that Muslim Spain was blindsided by religious vandals. Al-Mutamid, the Muslim governor of Seville, needed to fortify his principality against Alphonso, the menacing Christian king of Castile. To keep Alphonso at bay, al-Mutamid solicited the help of some iron-fisted Muslims from Morocco, the Almoravids. True to form, the Almoravids took care of Alphonso, but then they took over in a rampage of theological purity, something al-Mutamid never expected. The Almoravids hated the liberties of Muslim Spain, which they viewed as the result of unholy creative license. They despised Jews, deplored women, abhorred debate, and assumed a maniacal missionary position. Trust me, exiling Ibn Rushd doesn't begin to capture the scope of their lacerations. These troglodytes went further. Ever heard of al-Ghazali? He was a Baghdad-based thinker who accused liberal Muslim philosophers of "incoherence." A view the Almoravids could embrace, no? But al-Ghazali was himself declared too liberal by the Almoravids, who publicly torched his work. They also repressed the Sufis, Muslim mystics who read the Koran metaphorically rather than literally.

You know what I find instructive about this whole episode? That Muslim Spain didn't crumble because of ravenous Christians. Oh, sure, Christians scooped up the pieces, but the brutes who brought down Muslim Spain were Muslims. And you know what this suggests to me? That Muslims were imposing martial law and bludgeoning each other's freedoms *before* European colonialism took off. My point is, our problems didn't start with the dastardly Crusaders. Our problems started with us. To this day, Muslims use the white man as a weapon of mass distraction—a distraction from the fact that we've never needed the "oppressive" West to oppress our own.

I'll illustrate this point further by shifting focus to Baghdad. Remember the ninth-century caliph, al-Mamun? He espoused a version of Islam that promoted rational thought and eschewed any notion that the Koran had divine origins. Above all, al-Mamun's theology insisted on the free will of every human being. Right. In a stunning repudiation of both free will and rational thought, al-Mamun launched an all-out inquisition of officials who disagreed with his interpretation of Islam! Some objectors were flogged, others jailed. An heir to al-Mamun had at least one dissenter decapitated. Who else but Muslims can be held accountable for these atrocities? The Roman Church? Try again. The Jews? Sorry. MTV? Not yet. Guess who's left?

After three decades of forced "free will," first under al-Mamun and then under his nephew, another caliph reversed policy and cleared the field for a new dynastywide doctrine. This one decreed that believers must accept what the Koran stipulates "without asking how." In a nutshell, it's not for us to wonder how God can assert certain laws since we're utterly incapable of relating to Him—the Original, the Peerless, the Unfathomable. His revealed word stands for itself. It's our job to comply. Obviously, not everybody complied. Witness Ibn Rushd, along with any number of public blasphemers who preceded him. Still, looking around us now, it seems that this don't-ask-how orthodoxy triumphed. And it triumphed largely because it had the political tide in its favor. The spirit of independent thinking persisted in pockets of the empire, but the formal tradition of ijtihad was deliberately aborted. Feel free to ask how.

To answer, I need to set the scene by explaining that early Muslims feuded over who should succeed the Prophet in 632 C.E. Some pushed for his relatively young son-in-law and cousin, Ali. More Muslims endorsed Muhammad's elder companion, Abu Bakr. These blood-soaked squabbles precipitated Islam's first schism: the breakaway Shia ("faction of Ali") versus the majority Sunni (followers of the *Sunnah,* or tradition). For about 275 years, that division simmered. It flared up with a vengeance in 909 C.E., when a splinter group of Shias proclaimed a separate government within the Sunni-led Islamic empire. The Shias' upstart proclamation then inspired the ruler of Muslim Spain to announce his own, rival, claim to being "Commander of the

Faithful"—in short, the caliph. Amid so much chaos, the regime in Baghdad closed ranks.

Within a few generations, Baghdad oversaw the closing of something else—the gates of ijtihad and therefore the tradition of independent thought. In the guise of protecting the world-wide Muslim nation from disunity (known as *fitna* and considered a crime), Baghdad-approved scholars formed a consensus to freeze debate within Islam. These scholars benefited from patronage and weren't about to chirp an ode to openness when their masters wanted harsher lyrics. So, from their politically motivated perspective, everything Muslims needed to know was known. Got a new question? The four existing Sunni schools of thought can address it. They've never dealt with a question as novel as yours? Then they'll imitate past verdicts. No trailblazing tolerated.

We in the twenty-first century live with the consequences of this thousand-year-old strategy to keep the empire from imploding. But I've got news for you: The Islamic empire no longer exists. I'll say it again. The empire's gone. We're here. And the gates of ijtihad—our minds—remain, for the most part, closed. Why should this be? Why do mainstream Muslims continue to suppress their brainpower when the stated aim of the no-thinking rule—to preserve the integrity of Muslim lands from Iraq to Spain—is now a deafeningly moot point? Give your heads a shake, my friends. The only thing this imperial strategy has achieved is to spawn the most dogged oppression of Muslims by Muslims: the incarceration of interpretation.

Let me be more specific. As the gates of ijtihad closed, the right of independent thinking became the privilege of the *mufti,* the lawyer-priest, in each city or state. "To this day," says Mahmoud Ayoub, muftis "issue legal opinions, called fatwas, in accordance with the principles of their respective legal schools. Collections of famous fatwas have been made, which serve as manuals especially for less creative or less able muftis." Less creative? Less able? Than whom? You or me? Why do we need these guys at all? Rather than imitating their imitation of each other's rulings, shouldn't we be rattling the gates of ijtihad and ripping off the lock?

Take another example of how we venerate redundancy: Sharia law. Having been told that the Sharia represents Islamic ideals, most Muslims assume it's holy. Hooey. "[T]he bulk of the shari'ah," writes reform advocate Ziauddun Sardar, "is nothing more than the legal opinion of classical jurists"—in other words, those belonging to the four schools of Sunni thought. Constructed during the days of empire, these codes have been imitated ever since. "That is why," says Sardar, "whenever the shari'ah is imposed—out of context from the time when it was formulated and out of step with ours—Muslim societies acquire a medieval feel. We see that in Saudi Arabia, Iran, the Sudan, and Afghanistan under the Taliban."

Even where the Sharia doesn't seem to be operating, imitation still does. Recently, students at a university in Palestine tossed their professor out the window of their second-story classroom. His offense? Reinterpreting early Islamic history. He survived, but I'm not sure Palestine can survive the cream of its crop showing such deep disdain for inquiry. And then there's the pro-Chechen website that glorifies imitation in a slightly more elevated way. It bastardizes the genius of Maimonides to post a "Guide for the Perplexed on the Permissibility of Killing Prisoners." Imagine my relief when I learned that it *is* permissible (indeed, mandatory) to kill infidels—unless the imam or his deputy decides otherwise. Phew! At least I didn't have to think about it.

. . .

HAVING DISCOVERED HOW IMITATION CAME TO BE THE NORM IN Islam, I remained perplexed by something. If we're going to imitate, then why not imitate tolerance instead of tyranny? Didn't we have a healthy precedent to emulate—ugh, imitate—in the way Muslims worked with Jews and Christians during the golden age of Islam? Why, then, have so many of us slid into an apparently bottomless pit of poisonous feeling toward non-Muslims?

Asking these questions got me more than I'd bargained for. Because as I rummaged, I realized that Muslim tolerance of Jews and Christians has always been fragile. During the golden age, tolerance often resembled low-grade contempt, not acceptance.

There's an Egyptian-born European scholar who dumps cold water on any dreamy view of how Muslims have historically dealt with the "other." Bat Ye'or is her name. Actually, it's her pseudonym, adopted because what she argues drives a lot of Muslims into fits of fury. Ye'or coined the word *dhimmitude* to describe Islam's ideology of wholesale discrimination against Jews and Christians. Why *dhimmitude?* It comes from *al-dhimma,* the Arabic term for those groups—our fellow Peoples of the Book—who are entitled to protection in Muslim societies.

Protection? Let's home in on the premise behind this principle. Why would Jews and Christians need special protection if they're kindred People of the Book, deserving of rights and responsibilities equal to those of Muslims? That's the problem. Muslim societies have a hard time treating Jews and Christians (let alone anybody else) as equals in the dignity department.

An illustration: Under Muslim rule, Jews and Christians have historically bought their protection—in essence, paid for their lives—by handing over a poll tax. It's known as the *jizya,* and the Koran permits this tax in order to maintain the general peace. Not exactly a dignity-stoking practice, is it? Yes, Prophet Muhammad proved you can exercise free will here. When the general peace didn't appear to be jeopardized, he didn't impose the jizya. Still, the sheer option to levy such a tax screams "blackmail" to me.

Bat Ye'or's research amplifies the charge. Consider the terms that Muhammad reportedly dictated to a group of Jewish peasants after his soldiers looted their oasis at Khaybar, north of Medina. She writes, "The Prophet allowed the Jews to farm their lands, but only as tenants; he demanded delivery of half their harvest and reserved the right to drive them out when he wished." I'm not trying to pick on the Prophet; it's just that his conduct would have set the tone for realpolitik in Islam.

To be fair, other historians suggest that Muhammad showed an abiding admiration of his Jewish neighbors. He urged Muslims to join the fast that Jews performed on their day of atonement. He designated Friday, the start of the Jewish Sabbath, as the time for Muslim communal prayers. And he picked Jerusalem, not Mecca, as the original direction of prayer. Lovely gestures. But we have to confront this question: Is it possible that these were only gestures, offered up by an excellent politician, and that overemphasizing them distracts us from the malignant underside of Islam?

I'm pushing the question for a good reason. Not many years after the Prophet's death, a disturbing and supposedly authoritative document appeared. It decreed that non-Muslims must stand when any Muslim wishes to sit, that non-Muslims must watch their houses of worship decay without repairing or replacing them, that a Muslim's testimony in court trumps that of a non-Muslim. You get the grim picture. This document was called the "Pact of Umar." Who was Umar? Prophet Muhammad's second successor—a decent and thoughtful fellow by almost every account I've read. It's a mystery how his name came to be aligned (or maligned) with a series of such thoroughly suprema-cist diktats. And since that part isn't clear, the question comes up yet again: Why did Muslims choose intolerance over tolerance through the Pact of Umar? I made a "pact" with myself to keep this question on my radar.

For now, all I can tell you is that the Pact of Umar had a deci-sive effect on early Islam—and beyond. At the dawn of the ninth century, an eminent legal scholar used the pact as the basis for advising Muslim governors on what kind of relations they should seek with their non-Muslim subjects. The scholar drew up something of a boilerplate agreement. Have a glance at a few of the terms directed toward Jews and Christians:

- "You shall not occupy the middle of the road or the seats in the market, obstructing Muslims . . ."
- "You shall differentiate yourselves by your saddles and your mounts . . ."
- "You shall distinguish your headgear by a mark . . ."
- "You shall wear a girdle over all your garments, your cloaks and the rest, so that the girdles are not hidden . . ."

Imperialism, anyone? These regulations "were reinforced" by Muslim legislators and judges as a "divinely sanctioned system of discriminatory provisions," admits Abdulaziz Sachedina, a professor at the University of Virginia. Discriminatory. Divinely sanctioned. System. If no other word in that string strikes you, at least pause on "system." It calls to mind an entire culture of complicity. That's dhimmitude.

Throughout the five-hundred-year-long golden age of Islam, the Pact of Umar stood on the books, leading to the fragile tolerance I hinted at earlier. Let me flesh it out: Many Jews and Christians found themselves in a catch-22. They could politely decline their Muslim governor's request to take a public post, in which case they risked offending him, but if they accepted the invitation to serve, they risked being busted for violating rules of deference under the Pact of Umar, in which case their families and communities would pay, too.

Consider the example of Shmuel ha-Nagid and his son. Shmuel, you might recall, was prime minister to two Muslim kings in Spain. Despite being a creative juggernaut—poet, military commander, theologian—he brandished influence discreetly. Reuven Firestone of Hebrew Union College picks up the story: "When Shmuel died in 1055, his son Yosef was appointed to replace him. Although exceptionally talented, like his father, Yosef was arrogant and disliked. His lack of dhimmi comportment contributed to his downfall and he was eventually murdered in 1066 and the Jewish community of Grenada slaughtered. Technically, both Yosef and his father had broken the pact by accepting high public office and authority over Muslims. This fact was ignored when Shmuel comported himself with exceptional humility and when the kingdom as a whole was happy. However, when stress arose and Yosef refused to be self-effacing, his dhimma [protection] was breached. He was killed and his community devastated."

Still, Firestone asks us not to overlook "the relatively good position Jews and other religious minorities enjoyed under Islam." Plenty of scholars agree with him. One professor points out that in the Arab Muslim world of the Middle Ages, Jewish neighborhoods suffered no stigma, whereas in Christian Europe, the Church actively discouraged contact between Christians and Jews by restricting where each group could live. "Jewries," or Jewish-only streets, instilled "suspicion and dread into the popular imagination" of Christians. The scholar's point: Don't knock Islam because of a few massacres here and there. Instead, compare it to medieval Christianity, which sought to eliminate Judaism altogether.

I can accept this attempt at balance. But in the interest of even more balance, let's not trivialize the exquisitely mundane ways in which the Pact of Umar played out. In North Africa, Jews and Christians wore shoulder patches with pictures of pigs and monkeys, respectively. They had to slap these symbols on the doors of their homes, too. In Baghdad, seat of Islamic enlightenment, the dhimmi peoples dressed in clothes bearing yellow symbols—a marker resuscitated by the Nazis. I hope the pieces have started to fit for you. They did for me. I began to grasp how Islam has come to be an insular, often hateful religion. If you combine a ban on thinking with a long-practiced code of discrimination, what are you bound to get? You get imitation and you get intolerance. Above all, you get *imitation of intolerance.*

"Stop right there!" some of you may want to bellow. "How many times do I have to tell you that I'm not interested in humiliating Jews and Christians? I don't want them to wander around my town with yellow stars, okay? Don't implicate all Muslims in the 'imitation of intolerance.' Please." But the imitation of intolerance goes much deeper than yellow stars. No Muslim I know is entirely free from the system that supports it.

Since I'm calling for introspection, I'll use myself as an example. I grew up afraid of dogs because Islam taught me that dogs are dirty creatures. If you must use them as guards, hold your

nose. Under no circumstances should you pat one, let alone consider it a pet. And black dogs? They're demonic, pure and simple.
I was well into my twenties before I could touch a dog without
expecting a bite for trespassing against God.

This has a lot to do with the imitation of intolerance. In the
hadiths—the reports of Prophet Muhammad's sayings and
doings—nearly all mentions of black dogs appear alongside
degrading references to women and Jews. Far from being objective, these reports damn black dogs by associating them with
reviled "others." If we don't question the hadiths, and if we
don't open our eyes to patterns of prejudice, then we can easily
feed a system that treats millions of God's creatures as inferior,
even occult, beings.

It comes off as crazy, doesn't it? Yet the fallout is real. Listen
to the experience of a UCLA professor, Khaled Abou El Fadl.
He knows a Muslim convert who was instructed by a mullah to
ditch his pet dog. This convert found that no matter where he
left the dog, it would straggle back to his doorstep. The man
asked his mullah what to do with a dog who refused to be
abandoned.

Starve it, the mullah replied.

When El Fadl heard this merciless story, he was catapulted
into rebellion. The Kuwaiti-born, Egyptian-trained scholar of
Islamic law pored through original texts and early interpretations to find out if the mullah had any leg to stand on.
And that's when he discovered how dogs, women, and Jews
have been scurrilously linked as lesser beings, not by Prophet
Muhammad, who apparently thought highly enough of dogs to
pray in their presence, but by later intellects. Like the construct
of Sharia law, the vilification of dogs (and Jews and women) has
been a choice. God didn't choose it; a bunch of godfathers did.

Plenty of us buy into parts of their system, but we don't have to swallow any of it. El Fadl and his wife, Grace, have adopted three stray canines—one of them black. On top of that, Grace often leads the family prayer. Exercising ijtihad impels them to put the Creator's love over human laws.

LOOK, WE DON'T HAVE TO BE PRIZE-WINNING INTELLECTUALS TO exude the spirit of ijtihad. We need to express our questions about Islam openly. And we've all got questions cached away in our consciences.

From time to time, we've even acted on our questions. Timidly. Too timidly. A hundred years ago in Egypt, public discussions took place on Marxism, atheism, and the theory of evolution. According to one researcher, some fifty daily newspapers and two hundred weekly ones circulated freely, quoting strident secularists such as Voltaire. Calls for religious reform also surfaced. Catalyzed in the late nineteenth century by a political rapprochement with Europe, this intellectual renaissance eroded under anticolonialist rhetoric and the political pressures for Arab solidarity, which meant rejecting all things Western. But by the 1920s, most questions had faded to a whisper. Around this time, an Egyptian founded the Muslim Brotherhood, the Al-Qaeda of its generation. Rites of initiation into the brotherhood's terror cells featured two props: the Koran and a revolver. No questions asked.

A current example of this imitation of intolerence is the paranoid anti-Semitism that courses through Egypt. It's hard to know what to spotlight in such a short space, so let me illustrate by making you laugh. In the late 1990s, Israel volunteered to share farming technology with Egypt, living up to the biblical imperative to turn your swords into plowshares. Ah, peace. Except that the Egyptian press ran stories of toxic seeds and car- cinogenic cucumbers being handed out to unsuspecting farm- ers. The rumors got a lift from a homegrown campaign that accused Israelis of hawking two wicked products: chewing gum that threw ladies into spasms of lust, and genetically modified fruit that sapped their husbands' sperm. All this from an Arab country that has had a peace treaty with Israel since 1979!

Jordan is the only other Arab country to strike a peace deal with Israel. But several Jordanian newspapers, including at least two government dailies, have attributed September 11 to "the Jews." Read what another Jordanian paper saw fit to print, as translated by the Middle East Media Research Institute: "The Jews in Europe thought to move to the U.S. so as to take absolute control of [American] capital, banks, stock market, media, and po- litical decision making in both houses of Congress, and thus it was. The Jews infiltrated the American army, particularly the Air Force, and they prepared their pilots to take the planes, know- ing that religion is not denoted in the identity cards of those joining the American military. Accordingly, the airplanes [were controlled] by the Jews, as were the press, radio, television, and money in the banks and the stock market. Thus they took control of political decision making. Why is Bush ignoring these facts, and announcing that an investigation will be con- ducted to reveal who is behind the events? They are the Jews, Bush!"

You know what chills me more than the fact that these sweep- ing conspiracies come out of a "moderate" Arab Muslim coun- try? It's the fact that these attitudes follow Muslims to the West. If I needed further evidence, I got it in a letter about my post– September 11 articles. "I regard myself as a liberal Muslim," began the correspondent, who then lit into me for "destroy[ing] all that I have worked for, and that other Muslims have done, to promote the right and true message of Islam." What was that "right and true" message? He neglected to say, too engrossed in revealing that Zionists run the mass media and that my columns are "popping up in Jewish organizations." This liberal assured me that "I am not telling you to do self-censorship. Yet when the views of a Muslim like yourself are used by non-Muslims and Zionists, you must rethink."

Mr. Right and True proved right about one thing. The Zionists did pay close attention to my published pleas for reform. As a journalist with a reputation for flinging open doors, I was invited to visit Israel in the summer of 2002. Mulling over the offer, an important distinction occurred to me. Muslims treat women as horribly as we treat Jews. Yet we don't hold women responsible for our geopolitical ulcers and our intellectual stagnation. Would a clearheaded look at Israel contain the passkey to Islam's reform?

I met the offer to go to Israel with two conditions: I must be allowed to ask any questions I wanted, and I had to help shape the itinerary. Of course, said my Zionist sponsor—I could, should, and would be a partner in the journey. So, I asked myself again, should I go?

I remembered Mr. Khaki, and the *Queer Television* viewers who blamed the homosexuality of Muslims on Jewish "pigs" and "dogs." I thought about the feminist who cited "what's happening to Muslims in Palestine" as an excuse to stay silent about the Taliban. And I bristled at the "liberal" Muslim who warned me that I should rethink calls for reform because Jewish organizations were watching.

With the Arab/Jewish passion play constantly in our faces, I decided I had to see for myself if Israel merited the immobilizing anger of Muslims. I'm talking about the anger that we exploit to exonerate ourselves for our own condition—even in the West, where we bathe in the freedom to scrutinize our actions as much as anyone else's. If we're going to reverse the intolerance of the Muslim mind, we have to whip off the blinkers and wonder: Is Israel truly the monster we make it out to be?

I had the Zionists book me a plane ticket.

4

GATES AND GIRDLES

"How difficult will it be to go to the Territories?" I asked Paul, a staffer with the organization sponsoring my trip to Israel. I was referring, of course, to the Occupied Territories—the West Bank and the Gaza Strip.

"Ooh," he murmured. "Difficult."

It was a heartbreakingly low point in the Israeli–Palestinian conflict. The peace process had completely combusted and a new *intifada* was raging. Suicide bombings by Palestinians were accumulating and Israel was retaliating with a reoccupation—illegal Jewish settlements, assault helicopters, checkpoints, curfews, and the demolition of Yasser Arafat's compound in Ramallah. Israel didn't need the extra burden of safeguarding foreigners, but neither did it want to be perceived as preventing journalists from documenting the other side. Without any prompting from me, Paul included visits with several Arab artists and intellectuals in the itinerary. All of them, I would discover, had no qualms about criticizing Israeli policies. Still, I had to go

to the Territories. The four journalists with whom I'd be travel-
ing felt the same way.

"Let's see what we can do," Paul said.

By the time I arrived at Toronto's airport for the flight to Tel
Aviv, we hadn't received a yes. But we hadn't been told no.

THE OFFICIAL FROM EL-AL, ISRAEL'S STATE AIRLINE, INTERROGATED
everybody. I stepped up to greet him. "Born where?" he began.

"Uganda," I replied, flashing my citizenship card with the
photo of a pixie refugee whom I figured nobody could resist.

"Uganda? I'm from India, you know."

"A South Asian Jew?" I responded playfully. "How'd that
happen?" He divulged the family history before getting serious
again. Which schools had I attended? Did I graduate from all of
them? Had I ever carried out "plans" for relatives, like delivering parcels or ferrying an incapacitated uncle from one country
to another? After the probing, he got really animated: "I recognize you from TV. Great show." He meant *QueerTelevision*. So I
pointed out my partner, Michelle, standing a few meters away,
looking concerned about the intensity of our conversation. He
smiled at her and wished me a pleasant journey.

Michelle then took my photo in front of a sign for the King
David Lounge (a name I found deliciously kitschy). We said our
good-byes, nerves and smiles melding. The smiles whispered,
"This is it!" The nerves whispered, "Could this be . . . it?"
Michelle wasn't neurotic to wonder: Not twenty-four hours later,
an Egyptian immigrant stormed the El-Al ticket counter in Los
Angeles and gunned down two people. Toronto flights bound for
Tel Aviv originate in L.A. Had I waited an extra day to fly, I likely

wouldn't have made it to Israel any time soon—Michelle wouldn't have let me go, and I wouldn't have blamed her.

While still processing the richness of an East African Muslim encountering a South Asian Jew, I got another hint of Israel's complexity. The flight's safety video, though narrated in Hebrew, had Arabic subtitles. Arabic is an official language in Israel. Who knew?

I landed without incident. The six-day trip would be split into two major blocks: the first couple of days would be spent in Israel's commercial center, Tel Aviv, the second leg in the spiritual capital, Jerusalem. As well, we would stop in smaller cities primarily populated by Arab Israelis and, along the way, I continued to hope, take time in the Territories. That's a frenetic amount of activity, I know. But on my first full day in Tel Aviv, I realized that Israelis breathe freneticism.

It's in the form of cultural fluidity. Over lunch, an Israeli journalist told me about a new production of *My Fair Lady* in Hebrew with an Arab woman playing the lead. "In the 1980s, there was an effort to establish a Palestinian National Theatre," he added. "All performances were in Arabic and the organizers actively invited Israeli theater critics to come. In fact, the theater gained a passionate following among liberal Jews, but it never really caught on with Palestinians." The theater faltered after its founders, a married couple, got divorced. However, it was the intifada that aborted exchanges between Arabs and Jews at the Tel Aviv Museum of Art, which we were about to visit.

A bit of background first. The museum developed in the 1930s, well before Israeli independence and at a time when camels could still be spotted in the streets. Persuaded that the town would become a city and that every great city must ally with artists, Tel Aviv's mayor wrote to collectors around the world for loans. German Jews, facing an uncertain future, sent their treasures to him. In that way, stunning sculptures and paintings escaped confiscation or outright obliteration. The story gets better. Art that was shared among Jews came to be enjoyed by Jews and Arabs. For much of the 1990s, the director of a gallery in Palestinian East Jerusalem displayed items from Tel Aviv's art collection and, in turn, lent the museum pieces that his own Arab community had created. At the height of the peace process, an Egyptian artist exhibited her work in Tel Aviv. The museum arranged for some of her installations to travel to Palestinian territories.

No longer. "We'd love to continue to work with him," the curator of the Tel Aviv Museum said of her Arab counterpart in East Jerusalem. Since the intifada, she had tried getting in touch, without success. "He's probably too frightened [of the Palestinian Authority] to have contact with us now." Probably? Why would she assume that? I prodded a smidgen, to no avail. Her soft-spoken manner made it seem rude to push. But I would soon return to her statement.

As I left the building, a visual contrast struck me. The low, sprawling stone edifice of the Tel Aviv Museum of Art sits directly across the street from the towering, spacelike headquarters of the Israeli Defense Forces. This juxtaposition of creativity and hierarchy might be coincidental, but it can be found everywhere in Israel—home to Hasidic political parties *and* the only annual gay pride parade in the Middle East. That point was made to me in one of my first conversations with an Israeli, the same journalist who told me about the Palestinian National Theatre and its Jewish following. He went on to pose the most existential and touchy of questions: Should Israel remain a "Jewish state" or should it evolve into a purely secular one where faith is incidental? And what role should the Holocaust play, not just in the official history of Israel but in its present-day identity as a place of refuge? Righteous, I thought, that an Israeli would be openly asking these things of himself, let alone of a stranger like me.

Throughout my stay, in fact, Israeli media passionately debated such questions. I didn't think you could assail religion in a Jewish state. I was wrong. I read about a secular member of the Knesset, Israel's legislature, who remarked that the country doesn't need more religious Jews from North America. One newspaper fanned his comments into a minor firestorm. He later claimed he'd meant "ultrareligious" Jews. Whatever. Israel's laws guarantee freedom of expression, and that says something.

I especially enjoyed reading newspaper editorials, whose choice of subjects indicated a ferociously free press. Take *Ha'aretz,* the *New York Times* of Israel. It skewered a government proposal to allocate state lands to exclusively Jewish towns. You know how *Ha'aretz* described this bill? "Racist." Right there in the headline, "A racist bill." No sugarcoating, no equivocating, no apologizing. The bill died under intense Israeli criticism.

I have to tell you about another controversy being reported in the papers during my trip. It revolved around the fairness with which foreign news networks were covering the Palestinian-Israeli conflict. Israel's communications minister threatened to pull CNN off the national airwaves and replace it with Fox. To which *Ha'aretz* responded: If you do, you're no better than Arafat, who once slammed down the phone on CNN's Christiane Amanpour. In a rousing defense of principle over propaganda, the most influential newspaper in Israel asserted, "It is the right of Israelis to know that CNN and the BBC are not mirror reflections of official Israel's point of view . . ."

Still reeling, I turned the page—only to come across more self-criticism. "Has Jewish history been sufficiently attentive to the accomplishment of its women leaders?" wondered the author. "Probably not . . ." She proceeded to tell the story of a Jewish banker named Dona Gracia Nasi, who rescued thousands from the Spanish Inquisition by parlaying her financial savvy into political clout. A few days after that article appeared, Israel applauded another female role model. For the first time, the military made a woman its chief spokesperson. I remember thinking that for all of Israel's ethical excavation (and maybe because of it), this is a society seemingly moving forward, even as it contends with religious literalism among its own.

Entering Jerusalem for the second half of my trip, I took in a scene from the car window. Fully uniformed, a young woman marched in front of a dozen male soldiers. Where was she leading her troops? I turned to my guide. He said they were heading into the Old City—the religious quarters of Jerusalem—"where they'll spend three days or so being educated about the various faiths represented here."

"You mean, religious literacy is part of military duty?"

"Sure. The army makes time, every few months, for soldiers stationed in Jerusalem to learn about traditions outside of their daily experience." I learned the value of this program in a personal way the next afternoon.

I'M SCHEDULED TO VISIT THE DOME OF THE ROCK. ISLAM'S third-holiest shrine can be instantly recognized for its golden roof, whose arresting shimmer surely encourages the sun to rise and set every day. Islamic tradition says that this mosque houses a special rock—the one that Prophet Muhammad climbed during the "Night of the Ascension." At the rock, Muhammad found a spiral ladder that carried him to heaven, where he mingled with, prayed beside, and took wisdom from earlier prophets. It's a story that makes me fall in love with Islam, defining my faith's potential for pluralism.

The Dome of the Rock stands on the platform of the Temple Mount, which Jewish tradition and plenty of archeologists claim was the location of the central temple in the ancient kingdom of David. It's also the spot where riots erupted in September 2000, launching the latest intifada. A few days before the uprising, Ariel Sharon had trekked to the Temple Mount. In the wake of a failed peace process that saw Israel offer to divide Jerusalem, Sharon suggested he was only trying to show that the Temple Mount esplanade remained open to Jewish worshipers. And as a friend of conservative Jews, he reckoned that such a visit would boost his as-yet-informal campaign to become prime minister. A cynical political pantomime. Speaking of cynical politics, Arafat's chief of security in the West Bank preapproved Sharon's visit. A Palestinian Authority cabinet minister later revealed that Arafat had been planning the intifada for months. He needed a provocation, and that's exactly how Sharon's excursion to the Temple Mount came off to Palestinians—as a provocation. The intifada began, and the iron gates to both the Dome of the Rock and a neighboring mosque, Al-Aksa, were shut tight to everyone but local Muslims. Since then, this part of old Jerusalem—once an attraction for Jews, Christians, and people of no organized faith—has been emptied of its ecumenical energy.

I show up at the gates in an opaque dress that reaches my ankles, along with a long-sleeved, buttoned-up cardigan. I'm loath to calm my spiky coif. Nonetheless, it's tamed by the hijab swaddling my head. The Israeli foreign ministry has already informed the caretakers of this site, a religious authority known as the Wakf, that I'm coming. The message: Don't give her too hard a time, gents; she's one of you.

Not quite.

A burly member of the Wakf looks me up and down. He denies having received any word from the ministry. My guide assures him it was conveyed. Wakf-man mumbles into his walkie-talkie and, in a few minutes, another bearish brother saunters over. I don't realize it at the time but the delay has nothing to do with official notice or lack of it. My name, Irshad, is unisex, and far more common among males than females. When the Israeli foreign ministry alerted the Wakf about me, I'll bet the boys assumed they'd be receiving a man.

Since I don't have a male Muslim escort, what to do now? The haggling ends when an officer with the Jerusalem police agrees to chaperone me inside the gates. But before I can step onto sacred ground, one further measure must be enforced. A Wakf member comes running with a girdle in hand and tells me to slip it on. Not yet exasperated, I begin to shimmy into the garment. "Nah, nah, nah!" I glance upwards to see a stubby finger wagging wildly. He wants the girdle over, not under, my dress.

Holy crap—the Pact of Umar strikes again! Wearing girdles over clothes is a condition with which all dhimmi people must comply. I, as a Muslim woman, am akin to a religious minority in the judgment of the Wakf. Hell, I might be an undercover Jew. More likely, though, I'm just plain inferior.

I clamp my tongue, tighten my hijab for the bumpy ride ahead, draw a deep breath, and rock my body side to side in hopes of cajoling the girdle past my hips. Hope springs eternal, but not *that* eternal. Through my chaperone, I tell Brother Fashion Fascist that the girdle won't fit over my dress. He scowls. I want to snarl back, "Deal with it!"

Wakf-man settles for the garment going under my dress. The nice Muslim boys stare unrepentantly as I gingerly wiggle into the thing. Thank God I decided to wear something else under my dress this morning—biking shorts.

With that embarrassment behind us, my chaperone and I walk through the gates. We move haltingly, as the girdle prescribes my pace. While the police officer accompanies me around the open-air platform that is the Temple Mount, he peppers our informal tour with bits of Islamic history. He used to be a soldier and remembers a lot of what he learned on his mandatory educational foray into the Old City. As for my specific questions, I would have to ask the Wakf. Can you say "Forget it" in Arabic? The Wakf won't even take my photo for the folks back home, never mind partake in conversation. Odd that it requires a Jew to welcome me here. Or, in light of our shared theology and centuries-old history with the Temple Mount, it might be entirely appropriate.

My police escort takes me to the doors of the Al-Aksa mosque. As I slip off my sandals, then adjust my hijab in preparation to enter, an elderly man pushes himself off the wall he's been leaning against and blocks my path. Both my chaperone and I try to assure him I've been approved, but either he doesn't understand us or he doesn't believe us. We call for the Wakf. Maybe it's the Buddhist in me, but I expect nothing from them and, as a result, I'm not disappointed. The Wakf won't confirm for the elderly man that they've opened the gates to me. A protracted, hollow pause ensues in which we all stand around looking every bit the fractious Muslim nation we are.

Then grandpa, squinting directly at me, spits out the first line of the first verse of the Koran. "Bismillah al-Rahman al-Raheem!" There's something about his inflection. Is he testing me to come up with the next line?

I furnish it snappily. "Al-Hamdulillah rabb al-Alameen!"

"Al-Rahman al-Raheem," he shoots back.

Years of madressa instruction have come to this, a prayer-off with an ornery old dude on the Temple Mount in Jerusalem. "Maliki yaum al-deen," I ricochet. After a couple more rounds, it's clear I've proven enough of my credentials that gramps will have to account to Allah for obstructing a Muslim's right to worship.

He reluctantly ushers me through—with one last condition. While inside the mosque, he says, I must relinquish my camera because photographing any creature who has a soul promotes idolatry. Hold up. Was it not Muslims who, in the golden age of Islam, pioneered optical imagery? Didn't their inventions influence nineteenth-century photography? I banish the thought; sanity dictates that I shut my beak and plunk my camera into my chaperone's hand.

The world inside Al-Aksa mosque is markedly different from grandpa's congealed cosmos. This sanctum is coed. No physical wall segregates men and women. I do notice that only one woman sits on the elegantly woven carpet, and that she keeps her distance from the sprinkling of male worshipers. But at least she's there, among them. Some of the men look sedate; others slump in exquisitely designed doorways or spread out on the floor, depleted by the afternoon heat. In part, that's why I don't feel watched as I stroll about.

Correction: I don't feel watched by self-anointed authorities. I am, however, being surveyed. In the far corner, a gaggle of boys giggles at this woman caressing the gorgeous columns and cocking her head in several directions as she looks up and around. The boys' teacher gently shushes them. I motion to the teacher gingerly, unsure if I'm courting trouble. He grins and greets me in Arabic, shifting to English when he realizes that's what I speak. "From where do you come?"

"Toronto."

"Ah, you're the one. Yes, we expect you." (So the Israeli foreign ministry *did* inform the Wakf! Thus the tip-off to a more political agenda at play in the stall tactics that I encountered at the gates.)

"Good, I'm glad I haven't surprised anyone." I seize on the obvious warmth between us. "Would you let me photograph you and your students, sir? It would mean a lot."

"No problem," he replies.

Aha! Not everybody agrees with gramps that capturing creatures on camera is tantamount to revering them. If a Koran instructor, in particular, can refrain from reducing scripture to such numbing banalities, maybe multiple interpretations exist even in this hotbed of Palestinian activism. The challenge is to express them without fear of retaliation.

For now, I've got a class photo to snap. Still girdled, I waddle out of the mosque, discreetly catch my chaperone's attention, reclaim the camera, and perform the dirty deed. As I thank the teacher and his boys, something catches my eye: One of the Koran students is wearing a T-shirt inscribed with Hebrew, the brand name of a local cola, I'm told. Anywhere else, and I wouldn't give it a second glance. At ground zero of the ongoing intifada, you better believe I do a double take.

My next station is the Dome of the Rock, where I find mostly women and children completing their prayers. I also find an interior that lacks the uplifting color of the Al-Aksa mosque. Maybe the enveloping dimness can be attributed to the spotlights streaming onto the rock in the middle of the mosque; by comparison, everything else looks dark. I approach the main attraction. Barricaded by high wooden railings, the rock's surface can barely be seen if you're short. I am. So I scavenge for something else that's compelling, and it turns out to be the candor of a woman in this mosque.

A school principal living in New Jersey, she was born in Jerusalem and returns frequently to visit her sister. During our chitchat, the principal learns that I'm in television and that I'd like to come back to shoot a series. "Please," she implores, "hire people from our [refugee] camps to help you. If they don't know about video cameras or microphones, you can teach them."

I quip that TV production is like Israeli-Palestinian politics— a ridiculously complicated process for a reasonably simple result. She misses the joke, distracted by the crisis at hand. "Our people are desperate. There are no jobs. There haven't been for a very long time."

"But what about all the foreign aid the Palestinian Authority gets from the West?" I counter. I don't bother to bring up additional monies from a United Nations relief agency that's been devoted to Palestinian refugees for three generations now. "We're talking millions of dollars that can be used for labs and hospitals and schools and business enterprise zones. Why do you still have refugee camps? Where does all the aid go?"

"I don't know about all of it, but some of it . . ." She gestures as though placing cash into a pocket.

"Corruption?"

"Look over there," she mutters, motioning to a badly gashed

pillar in the mosque. "Muslims don't even have the money to maintain this beautiful place."

"Wait a minute," I reply, just a tad tartly. "Is it that we don't have the money, or that we don't have the leadership to use the money for the right things?"

"God knows." Actually, the answer arrives in her next breath. "Some people say, 'Don't worry as long as the mosque looks strong and sturdy on the outside.' They only care about the symbolism, not the people."

The afternoon has elapsed and I've got one more stop before I'm due for dinner. I hastily take photos—of women, of the pillar, of children, of the rock—and then leave, feeling as constricted by a sense of internal injustice as by the godforsaken girdle. My chaperone deposits me at the gate where it all began. This time, I shuffle behind a small, squat building to rid myself of the gnawing garment. I'll happily give it back to the Wakf. What I won't give them is a second chance to leer.

NOBODY HARASSES ME AT THE WESTERN WALL. I'M WELL AWARE that Jewish women fight their own battles to pray on equal terms with men. Some women have been spat at, even physically assaulted at the Wall. Court cases are still being waged. Fresh from my experience with the Wakf, I'm just grateful that no one ogles me at the wall. Or orders me into the linen equivalent of duct tape. Or pursues a chapter-and-verse showdown with me. The blood rush of being overwhelmed is all that intimidates.

The Western Wall is the stone facade whose innumerable crevices hold bits of paper inscribed with the prayers of Jews from all over the world. They flock to face the wall because, according to Jewish belief, it's the only remnant of the community temple that once stood where the Dome of the Rock now does, on the Temple Mount. Solomon, son of the Hebrew King David, erected a temple to be the center of the ancient Israelites' sacrifices to God. Babylonians destroyed that First Temple and Jews built their Second Temple around 515 B.C.E.. In 70 C.E., Romans sacked Jerusalem, leveled the Second Temple, and expelled the Jews from their kingdom. For centuries, Christians let the Temple Mount deteriorate as a testament to Judaism's downfall. But, as you know, Muslims eventually took the holy city. They refurbished the Temple Mount by putting Islamic imprints on it—first the Al-Aksa mosque, then the Dome of the Rock. Even though Muslims reopened Jerusalem to Jews, the Second Temple remained a shambles. Muslims never restored it. And to Orthodox Jews, that's as it should be: Reconstructing the temple is the job of the Messiah, for whom they're still waiting. Until then, the Western Wall serves as the nucleus of Jewish community—a roofless reminder of the past, of the future, of power, and of humility.

I get there fairly fast because the wall adjoins the Muslim quarter of Jerusalem. At first, I'm amazed that Muslim-Jewish interdependence exists even in the structural design of the Temple Mount. Later, I come across a newspaper article chronicling what a hassle this interdependence is for Jews who must beg the Wakf to fix water leaks in the Western Wall. For the sake of peace, you see, Israel has accorded Muslims the lion's share of authority in maintaining the Temple Mount. We're not talking sovereignty, just administrative control. Muslim control reaches all the way to the wall and encompasses just about everything behind it, like the damaged pillar in the Dome of the Rock. You can blame the Israeli occupation for many wounds. But not that one.

I borrow a pencil and scrawl a request to God, then weave

through the crowd to approach the wall. As I spend time in search of an unused crack that will clasp my prayer, I realize I'm holding up the Jews behind me. Still, I don't feel like an interloper. I feel at home. More viscerally than ever, I know who my family is.

Tell me I'm saccharine, but understand this much: When I say "family," the picture in my mind isn't of Prophet Muhammad or even of Abraham, it's of a toddler I ran into—actually, he ran into me—earlier in the day. While making our way to the Dome of the Rock, my guide took me through the Jewish residential quarter of the Old City. We stepped into a dank gathering place carved from stone and reverberating with the shrieks of children. They were climbing up and jumping off ruins. My guide said this was a playground to which Orthodox mothers felt safe bringing their toddlers, especially after *yeshiva* (religious school). Seconds later, a boy in a *kippa,* curly locks dangling from his temples, and the strands of his prayer shawl peeking out over his baggy black pants, turned the corner and plowed into me. He was steering a sleek, silver scooter—yet another illustration of a society on the move, propelled by its paradoxes. If even Jewish literalists don't have to insulate themselves from modernity, how much more opportunity to choose and fuse passions must mainstream Israelis enjoy?

When I spoke about this with great enthusiasm to a secular Israeli friend, she shared a personal story. Having grown up in Britain, detached from her Jewish heritage, Isabel opened herself to just about every adventure upon arriving in Israel as a teenager. That's how she got "picked up" at the Western Wall by an Orthodox Jew who offered free study at a yeshiva. Sounds creepy to cautious personalities, but Isabel's a pistol. She went. "The atmosphere was great," she told me at an Italian restaurant in Jerusalem. "People were generous and genuine and they encouraged me to ask questions. 'Keep asking,' they would nudge. Eventually, they couldn't answer my questions, so they sent me to the rabbi. After a couple of weeks, I decided I'd gotten the point of the yeshiva and left for something else to do. It was a wonderful experience. Nothing sinister at all." Today, as a senior correspondent for *The Jerusalem Report* magazine, Isabel commands the public recognition of a rising journalistic star.

I appreciate that not every yeshiva lives up to hers. Jim Lederman, Israel's longest-serving foreign correspondent, adds vital perspective. He writes that "the ultra-Orthodox rabbis have forbidden their followers to use the Internet because of what they may learn from it. And they very recently agreed to the establishment of what they called a university. But . . . they have specifically forbidden the study of history, literature, sciences dealing with evolutionary theory such as biology and astrophysics, and philosophy." I'll go further on the perspective front. The pressure to conform will always assert itself, everywhere. It's part of the human condition, I suspect. What Israel tries to do differently, as a society, is what I respect. Israeli society endows citizens with the permission to inquire and accumulate experiences. Here, a feminist can sue the government for equal access to the Western Wall. Here, a teenage girl can conceive of leaving her yeshiva without stigma. Here, too, a Hasidic boy can zip around on an emblem of consumer cool. Here, then, a people will witness their potential to be many things at once, reflecting the multitudes of God Himself.

THE TRIP TO THE TERRITORIES IS ON! WELL, ONE TERRITORY anyway—the West Bank. At breakfast, we're briefed by a diplomat who works directly with the Palestinians. He believes in them. "This is a people who, if left to themselves, are capable of governing themselves," he states. However, "left to themselves" means more than ending the military occupation by Israel. He hints that it also means replacing the imperious rule of the Palestinian leadership with a government that gives a damn about what its constituents want, no matter how distasteful to the nationalist cause. "Palestinians have learned a lot from Israel; in many ways, they want to emulate Israelis," the diplomat confides as we pile into his bulletproof vehicle. "My driver once told me, 'What we need here is rule of law, just like they have in Israel.'" Public opinion echoes him. According to the Palestinian pollster Khalil Shikaki, "When Palestinians are asked what democracy they most admire and want, to this day Israeli democracy comes first."

Our diplomat seems to feel that he's already said too much. Jittery by temperament, cagey by training, he falls quiet during the half-hour ride to Ramallah. It's not like there's nothing to discuss. Outside our first checkpoint, we brake at a traffic light. On the shoulder of the road stands a massive billboard slathered with pictures of babies. A line of Arabic script projects some sort of slogan. I ask the diplomat, who's chauffeuring us himself this morning, to translate. He pretends not to hear, then not to see, and finally cranes his neck to "get a closer look," by which point the light changes and we speed away. This wouldn't be the only dodge of the day.

We've come to Ramallah on a day when the Israeli army has lifted its curfew so that secondary school students can take their exams. The streets teem with shoppers, racing against time to stock another week's worth of rations. A horse-drawn carriage is parked between an old Jaguar and a new Audi. "Financed by the European Commission," say the signs on various building developments that resemble shacks. They're dilapidated and, in some cases, boarded up. We pull into a muddy side road, at the end of which is our destination, a diplomatic mission. From the outside, it's virtually anonymous, while inside, its vibe is anemic.

Yet I can't help but feel a twinge of anticipation. Among the Palestinian activists we're there to meet is Raja Shehadeh, a writer, lawyer, and founder of the nonpartisan human rights organization *Al-Haq* ("fairness"). I've asked for his presence because, at least in print, he's more than a gesticulating finger that's battery-operated to blame the "other." On the page, Shehadeh exudes nuance. I'm hoping to chat with him about his latest book, *Strangers in the House: Coming of Age in Occupied Palestine.* The book contains a portrait of his father, Aziz, the first prominent Palestinian to accept Israel's existence and advance a solution based on two states. According to Shehadeh, Arafat's henchmen responded to Aziz by branding him "a despicable collaborator" on Arabic radio. "You shall pay for your treason," the husky voice decreed. "We shall eliminate you. Silence you forever. Make an example of you for others." The Palestinian lawyers' union disbarred Aziz. Years later, he was mysteriously murdered. I figure that having his name on such a bold book signals Shehadeh's willingness to talk more about these native barricades to peace.

He isn't in the building when we arrive, but two other activists are. The first, Dr. Ali Jirbawi, a political scientist, dispenses a lengthy history lecture, then coaxes us with heartfelt reasoning. "Let's not kid ourselves. There is no such thing as a benign occupation. An occupation means that you lose control of your destiny. You saw in the checkpoints you went through that we cannot move." These checkpoints do, indeed, amount to a constellation of cages for Palestinians.

(From that perspective, the newly built security barrier is just another chokehold. Sections of it cut Arab villages into half, forcing merchants to use scrawny, nimble children as couriers of goods and messages. Children are the only ones who can squeeze through the clumsy gaps between the concrete slabs of the barrier. This can't be good for the Palestinian economy—or for Palestinian dignity.)

Stop the suicide bombings, a journalist in the room says, and everyone will have their movement back. Dr. Jirbawi disputes that Palestinians had much freedom of movement before the explosions became epidemic. He pulls a green pass out of his breast pocket. "I carry this with me wherever I go. In a different town, they carry another color. Our license plates are differently colored. It's apartheid." Then why, interjects someone else, did Arafat walk away in the summer of 2000 from the best chance ever for an independent state—a plan brokered by U.S. president Bill Clinton to grant Palestinians the vast majority of their demands? Dr. Jirbawi decries the offer as a deception, intended to recreate the Bantustans, or quasi-independent colonies, prevalent in apartheid-era South Africa. Even if that's true, we ask, why didn't Arafat counteroffer? Why did he simply reject the process and eject his people from the possibility of further negotiation?

Amid an exchange heaving with tension, Raja Shehadeh tiptoes into the room. He keeps a low, almost sullen, profile. Abdul-Malik Al-Jaber, the activist who's been at Dr. Jirbawi's side all along, speaks up to ensure that the apartheid theme doesn't vanish in the volley of our challenges. "My wife has a Jerusalem ID and when she gave birth to our daughter in Israel proper . . ." He details the bureaucratic runaround of applying for his newborn's health insurance, the moral of his story being that apartheid conditions blight Arabs throughout Israel, not merely in the West Bank and Gaza Strip. "We're residents of

Jerusalem and we pay all our taxes," he says, "but there are ways to deny us our rights, based on ethnicity."

He's right. Being a democracy doesn't stop any country from putting its minorities at a disadvantage. Look, for example, at how many more army recruiters than college scouts visit U.S. high schools that have lots of Hispanic students. Israel, too, is no stranger to perpetrating racism, as *Ha'aretz* would be the first to point out. However, after a three-month rigmarole, Al-Jaber and his wife *did* manage to register their daughter for health insurance. So were their rights ultimately denied? This isn't hair-splitting, not if you're going to accuse a government of practicing apartheid.

But I've got more immediate questions. Two of the three Palestinians have dutifully delivered their lines; will the third do the same? Or will we hear something—anything—about how the crisp dichotomies of us-against-them, Jew-against-Arab, parody both peoples? All eyes look to Shehadeh. Sheepishly, he brings out his book. "Attaboy!" I cheer silently.

"Page one seventy-three," Shehadeh announces. His recitation begins. "Ideology and bulldozers are the bane of this land. The first inspires and the second makes possible in a day what used to take a score of men a month to accomplish." Shehadeh uses the next several minutes to deliver a passage about the technology—and agenda—possessed by Israel to dispossess Palestinians. Having read his book twice and practically memorized key paragraphs, I notice that, in this situation, Shehadeh stops just before he reaches a significant section. It's a section in which his father says that a tenable solution for Palestine would have to be bargained, not bombed, into being. To quote precisely, "only a political initiative" will work. "And soon. Before there is no land left to speak of." A political initiative, and soon: exactly what Arafat had the opportunity to pursue and didn't.

I'm stunned by where Shehadeh wraps up. Still, I know enough about how this particular passage ends to understand why an otherwise robust intellectual would censor himself in front of two compatriots. In Palestine, he writes elsewhere in the book, "society conspires to destroy, discourage, and bring down by rampant corrosive jealousy those who triumph. It's a society that encourages you to cringe. Most of your energy is spent extending feelers to detect public perception of your actions, because your survival is contingent on remaining on good terms with your society." I'm reminded of what the Tel Aviv curator mentioned to me: It's probably out of self-preservation that her Palestinian counterpart won't return her calls. Any refusal to play along with collective victimhood comes at a steep cost, which Shehadeh's father paid in spades. "He was an energetic, public-spirited man who was never allowed to succeed. He had become a marked man . . ." I want to ask his son if that's how he perceives himself, too. But the question feels cruel. It's significant enough that on a morning when the people of Ramallah can roam, Raja Shehadeh doesn't dare venture beyond the hallways of half-truth.

Our meeting finishes abruptly, as the Palestinians remember they've got only so much time to run errands before the curfew is reinstated. We file out of the room, hungry and just a little perturbed that the organizers have prepared ham-and-cheese sandwiches for lunch. Ham and cheese! For a group of journalists that includes one Muslim and a couple of Jews. Served up at a den of diplomacy. Duh.

During our impromptu huddle about what else to do for lunch, I break away to peruse the materials in a magazine rack.

It holds studies, reports, and academic journals from the mid-1990s. I stuff a couple of publications into my bag because I can learn context from them, and, oh yes, I'm nosy. My nosiness is why I also love poking around airport bookstores. They're an index of what ideas a society will permit people to take away.

That night, before the flight home to Toronto, I enter Ben Gurion Airport with Ramallah on my mind—and an intention to find books on sale about the Palestinian-Israeli mess. I see only two: one that's relatively neutral, the other famously sympathetic toward Arabs. Israel allows its legitimacy to be questioned by histories that are marketed at its national airport. Go figure. And yet, I can't shake the allegation of apartheid hurled so vigorously by Palestinian activists in the West Bank. Day in and day out, they witness what I've only glimpsed: young Israeli women and men with guns strapped to their chests. Miles of dusty road to tread between checkpoints. Brusque soldiers who won't utter a word of Arabic, even if they know how. ID cards, razor wire, armored tanks, sprawling Jewish settlements that look like suburbs and would take years to dismantle, delaying justice for Palestinians that much longer. I'm thrown for an ethical loop. But I'm about to be enlightened.

On the flight, I open one of the publications I took from Ramallah, an issue of the *Journal of Palestine Studies*. It's dated 1997, a year when the peace process still held promise. The first article points out that those who founded Israel did so by suppressing democracy. The author quotes Chaim Weizmann, a Zionist leader, admitting that "we could not rest our case on the consent of the Arabs; as long as their consent was asked, they would naturally refuse it." The more I read of this article, the more I understand its author's bitterness.

In the same publication, I read the "confessions" of a man

who returns to Gaza after years away. In 1997, it looked as if an independent Palestine would be achieved, and he had come home to plan life after liberation. What he found, however, was a society blanched of honesty, grasping at every excuse to vent old grievances. "There were the newly whitewashed walls . . . walls which, only a few days later, after a Palestinian was killed by a stray Israeli bullet, were plastered with obituaries composed by all the known and obscure organizations claiming him as a hero and martyr and threatening terrible vengeance on his killers. Truth and the gleaming white walls were sacrificed, for it is certain that the victim belonged to none of those organizations. The thirst for martyrs is consuming, a dominant passion."

So, even at a time of relative optimism, the death wish had seized Palestinian Muslims. Why? Our confessor observes that it "wasn't just the harshness of the occupation," but a total absence of introspection as well. This triggered a "collapse of the values on which the social contract rests. Elevating oneself above criticism is not so much self-confidence as a sign of encapsulating oneself, closing oneself off from the rest of the world. The price has been exorbitant."

I resolve to learn more about how Muslims have broken faith with the Koran's warning that "God changes not what is in a people until they change what is in themselves." The Israeli press reassured me that there's no shame in airing communal frailties. The Wakf showed me there's plenty of disgrace in remaining gagged—by girdles or anything else. To hell with the gaggers. What else aren't we Muslims telling ourselves so we can keep surfing on sympathy and subsisting on victimhood?

5

WHO'S BETRAYING WHOM?

A joke circulating among Palestinians goes something like this. Arafat dies a martyr and reaches paradise. There, he finds a crush of kindred martyrs, eager to claim their virgins and vino, congregating outside heaven's door. The angels have denied them entry.

When the fed-up throng sees Arafat, they breathe a sigh of relief. "Our president is here and he will intervene," they console each other.

Arafat is befuddled. "Why aren't you inside?" he asks.

"Our names aren't on the lists," his boys report. "They don't have such things as Palestinians." So Arafat sidles up to the window and introduces himself to the angel-clerk as the leader of the Palestinian people.

"Who?" wonders the administrating angel.

"The Palestinian people," Arafat growls.

The angel-clerk combs through all lists of eligible entrants, and shrugs his regrets. Arafat demands to see God. The angel goes inside to tell God that someone's at the door and he's shouting that he and his people are martyrs and want their rightful place in paradise. "But," the angel points out, "they're not on the list."

"Are you sure?" God asks.

"I don't know how many times I've checked," the beatific bureaucrat answers.

God thinks a long while, then makes a decision. "Why don't you have the Angel Gabriel build them a camp until we find a proper solution for them."

Insert laughter. In heaven, as on earth, the Palestinians are perennial refugees.

This joke speaks to the Palestinians' sinking feeling that nobody wants them, not even the vaunted Arab "nation." You might call Palestinians the Jews of the Arab world.

THE MOVEMENT TO ESTABLISH THE STATE OF ISRAEL, A MOVEMENT known as Zionism, sprouted in Europe during the late 1800s. Zionists realized that anti-Semitism wasn't going away and might just be getting worse. Jews, they warned, needed a national homeland. And Jews needed it not in the Antarctic, nor in Uganda, but in the Near Eastern strip of sand and soil to which they traced their earliest, deepest, and most persistent roots—the land that Arabs belatedly minted Palestine.

There's a lot of controversy over whether Jews have a historical attachment to Palestine, and therefore whether they can call any of it a homeland. I think they can. First, according to a DNA study conducted by an international team of researchers and published in the *Proceedings of the National Academy of Sciences,* Jews and Arabs share at least one ancestor—a "common Middle Eastern origin," as the study puts it.

Islamic tradition concurs. It says that Ishmael, who established the Arab nation, and Isaac, who founded the Jewish nation, were half-brothers sired by Abraham. Prophet Muhammad reportedly descended from Ishmael, while Moses and Jesus came from Isaac's side of the family. All had a blood tie to Abraham. And if that's not enough for you, then listen to the Koran. "We said to the Israelites: 'Dwell in the land. When the promise of the here-after comes to be fulfilled, We shall assemble you all together.'" I hate to be selective, but not mentioning this verse would be selective too.

Finally, let's go back to the Zionist movement. When European Jews arrived in Palestine, they discovered a smattering of their coreligionists already living in what today would be the West Bank. When did Jews get there? Might Jews have always been there? Recent settlers in the West Bank tend to attract the most consternation, and often deserve to because of their illegal out-posts. But somewhere here is a homeland. To squawk that Jews are alien usurpers of Palestine is as ignorant as to rant that Arabs have no place in Israel.

How, then, did Palestinians become refugee outcasts, even within the Arab world? Through the disruptions of war—a conflict initiated by Arab countries that couldn't accept Israel's existence in their midst. Only one day after the birth of the Jewish state in 1948, five Arab armies invaded Israel, and the Palestinian refugee problem got serious. In some towns Israeli commanders expelled Arabs, egged on by a controversial strat-egy called the Dalet Plan. The grief it imposed can no longer be denied. In other towns, though, Arabs were urged to stay—and many stuck around to accept Israeli citizenship. Many more Palestinians chose to go, fully expecting to be back once the Jews had been driven into the sea.

And these refugees took their marching orders not from Israelis, but from Arabs. So said Khaled al-Azm, the prime minister of Syria during this war. In his 1973 memoirs, al-Azm wrote about "the call by the Arab Governments to the inhabitants of Palestine to evacuate it and to leave the bordering Arab countries, after having sown terror among them. . . . Since 1948 we have been demanding the return of the refugees to their homes. But we ourselves are the ones who encouraged them to leave." To al-Azm's chagrin, "[t]his collective flight helped the Jews, whose position improved without any effort on their part." So much for Israel being completely on the hook for the Palestinian refugee crisis.

The UN has also contributed to the crisis. Today, it considers 3.5 million Palestinians to be refugees, but it applies a definition that's given to no other displaced people. That definition includes not only the original refugees, who numbered about 700,000, but also their children and grandchildren. One third of them live in urban "camps" surrounded by high-rises, open fields, and private Palestinian villas.

Sad and unnecessary. After all, hundreds of thousands of Jews found themselves kicked out of Arab lands by the 1950s, yet they didn't languish in refugee holding tanks because Israel absorbed and integrated the vast majority of them. For that matter, Israel has granted citizenship to 98,000 Palestinians under a family reunification effort. What have Arab governments by and large done for Palestinians? According to Khaled al-Azm, "we have caused them to be barren and unemployed, though each one of them had been working and qualified in a trade from which he could make a living."

Recent history isn't much more impressive. After the 1991 Persian Gulf War, Kuwait banished at least 300,000 Palestinians from inside its borders as payback for Yasser Arafat's support of the invading Saddam Hussein. Most of the evicted "never knew Palestine or any country other than Kuwait," notes Kanan Makiya, author of a book about cruelty and silence in the Arab world. Besides booting out innocents, he says, "semi-official vigilante groups" in Kuwait "arbitrarily arrested" other Palestinians. "If they did not 'disappear' it was because they had been gunned down in public or tortured and killed."

Here's another barometer of Arab hypocrisy. For years, Kuwait donated less than Israel to the UN agency that cares for Palestinian refugees. Nor did Saudi Arabia outspend Israel until oil revenues gushed forth. And today? Despite obscenely over-stuffed money vaults and a whole lot of land to spare, the Saudis won't take in Palestinians as citizens. They will, however, broadcast telethons to raise millions for the financing of suicide bombers. They'll also award the families of successful bombers a trip to Mecca, all expenses paid.

In the surrounding countries of Lebanon, Syria, and Iraq, governments act as if settling Palestinians would upset a fragile coexistence between Shia and Sunni Muslims. In the case of Iraq, "coexistence" has meant that a Sunni minority ruled over the Shia majority. Why risk publicizing that fact by conferring citizenship on foreigners, no matter how Arab they may be? Like his nemeses in the House of Saud, Saddam expressed his concern for the Palestinians by subsidizing bombers' families. (The Great Uncle, as he liked to be called, sped up payments the week before the spring 2003 war in Iraq.) Lebanon could care even less. Its laws actually prohibit most Palestinian refugees from working full-time, purchasing land, or becoming professionals. They get by on odd jobs. Indeed, the only Arab Muslim country that has accorded citizenship to Palestinian refugees is Jordan, and that's because most Jordanians are ethnically Palestinian anyway.

We can rip into Israeli "imperialists" for the Palestinian plight. The truth is, though, that Muslims have our own imperialists to indict. Not in equal measure, you may say. Maybe in greater measure, I say. Parsing how the Mideast drama even started is a lesson in the ways that Muslims have been sticking it to each other for decades. *What I'm about to lay out isn't a comprehensive history, but a sampling of facts lost in the present polarization.*

In the early twentieth century, we conveniently believe, Zionists stomped in and turfed out Palestinians by force of arms. As I've said, plenty of Arabs did get the heave-ho. But the instructions to vacate didn't always originate with Jews. The Ottomans—Turkish Muslims—oversaw the empire that controlled Palestine at the time. Against the interests of Arab tenant farmers, the Ottomans voluntarily sold land to the early Zionists. Yes, Muslims did this. And they did it consciously. In 1911, 150 high-profile Arabs telegraphed the Turkish parliament to protest continued land sales. Their cable was ignored.

During the First World War, the Arabs helped Britain fight the Ottomans on condition that all of Palestine would be turned over to the Arabs afterwards. Sir Henry McMahon, Britain's high commissioner for Egypt and Sudan, appeared to call it a deal in a series of private letters in 1915. Yet, in the Balfour Declaration of 1917, Britain broke its presumed pact with the Arabs. London publicly committed some of Palestine to the Jews, who were facing increasingly spiteful attacks in Europe. Thus the Promised Land became the twice-promised land. Muslims have cursed Western colonizers for treachery ever since.

Once again, though, we've failed to atone for our own travesties of 1915. That year marks the height of the Ottoman Muslim genocide perpetrated against Armenian Christians. Allah's ambassadors expunged more than a million Christians through deportation, starvation, and bloodbaths. Why don't I hear too many of us calling on the Turks to make amends? We should be indignant, particularly since Armenians seek back none of their property—only an apology. Are Muslims too busy cleaving to the sanctimony of the betrayed to care about how we're betraying others?

We Muslims aren't the only ones who had to settle for less from colonial powers; Jews also experienced betrayal. The year was 1921. Of the land that Britain designated for the Jewish national home, almost four-fifths went to Arabs for what would become Jordan. Only two years later, Britain ceded more Jewish-slated territory, this time to Syria. But then, as now, the concessions foisted on Jews meant nothing to delusional Muslims.

Are you familiar with the name Haj Amin el-Husseini? You should be. He became the mufti of Jerusalem in 1921 and president of the Supreme Muslim Council in 1922. Though Haj Amin had been properly elected to the council, ballots would never be cast again during his fifteen-year presidency. Through his single-minded intent to rid Palestine of the Jews, the mufti also revealed himself to be morally content with authorizing the serial murder of Arabs. Those who got in his way got in God's way. As the Nazi menace swelled in Europe, so did Jewish migration—and Haj Amin's tyranny. "For an Arab to be suspected of a lukewarm adherence to the national cause is to invite a visit from a body of gunmen," noted the British government's 1937 Peel Commission Report on civil unrest in Palestine. The report added that "a number of Arabs have asked for [British] Government protection." Blaming the Jews for the "inner terror" of Arabs would be yet another lie.

What came next is a part of history that you rarely hear mentioned these days. In 1939, drained by mounting disturbances in the Middle East and anxious to focus on defeating Hitler, Britain offered the Palestinians a plan for full statehood. The terms: Arabs and Jews would inhabit a single polity, to come under Palestinian control in ten years. Meanwhile, Jewish land purchases and Jewish immigration would be dramatically cut. Upon independence, the Palestinians could decide their own immigration policy. By any standard, that's autonomy. Not sweet enough, said Arab representatives. Swayed by the mufti of Jerusalem, whom Britain wouldn't talk to directly, the Arab negotiators wanted liberation in half the time. Otherwise, London could shove it.

But it's the ordinary sods who got royally shafted. In rejecting Britain's gesture, the mufti's men never consulted the farmers and merchants of Palestine. The people, it appears, took issue with the elite agenda. According to a 1938 British newspaper story, most villagers "have no great sympathy with the Arab rebels who are trying to stem the tide of Jewish immigration and demanding an Arab Government for Palestine. They merely want to be left alone to sow and harvest; to marry and find the wherewithal in these troubled times to bring up their families." Politically impoverished by their own chieftains, Palestinians found themselves economically deprived, too. Eight former Palestinian commandos published a manifesto charging the mufti of Jerusalem with misusing "the inestimable sums of money received from foreign powers. These are millions of pounds, but can Haj Amin at least point to a single mosque, a school, or a hospital he erected during this period? Did he build a shelter or an asylum or a charity or a cistern from which poor tramps could drink?"

Let's be straight about what else happened during the Nazi years: Muslim complicity in the Holocaust. Haj Amin, the same godly guy who practiced his assassination skills on Arabs, pressured Britain to turn away boatloads of Jewish refugees bound for Palestine. Some drowned in the Mediterranean; some were sent back to the gas chambers and crematoriums of Europe. The mufti pressed on, stopping Croatian children—many of them orphaned—from making it to the Holy Land. He nonetheless calculated that reducing the population growth of Jews wouldn't be enough to guarantee an Arab Palestine immediately after the war. For this, the mufti needed to be known, trusted, and owed in the winner's circle. Betting and praying that this war's winner would be Hitler, Haj Amin paid the führer a personal visit. The mufti's blond hair and blue eyes became barometers of credibility, comforting Hitler that, in his own words, Haj Amin "may well be descended from the best Roman stock." The mufti wound up as Hitler's special guest in Berlin, presiding over the unveiling of the Islamic Central Institute in December 1942.

He also made sorties into the Balkans to draft Muslim volunteers for the Axis war effort. Some Bosnian Muslims not only resisted his charms, but actively hid Jews in their homes. (When Israel honored such a Bosnian family in the 1960s at a ceremony in Jerusalem, they decided to stay and become Israeli citizens.) Other Muslims from India, Central Asia and, yes, Palestine gave their lives to serve the Allied cause. But before we righteously proclaim that the Holocaust happened in Christian Europe, let's look harder into the mirror. Many Muslims hitched their futures to Hitler. In 1943, Haj Amin addressed imams in the Bosnian SS, assuring them that Islam and Nazism shared a commitment to social order, family structure, hard work, and perpetual struggle—especially against the Americans, the English, and the Jews. From the capital of the Reich, Haj Amin broadcast Nazi propaganda to the Arab world. "Kill the Jews wherever you find them," he hissed into a microphone at Radio Berlin on March 1, 1944. "This pleases God, history, and religion. This saves your honor. God is with you." Letters from Arab listeners to German diplomats in Baghdad and Beirut suggest the mufti's message had an impact.

Although he lost his gamble on Hitler, the mufti escaped the mantle of a war criminal. Arrested in France after the war, he smuggled himself out of Allied detention and eventually went to Egypt. The newly formed Arab League welcomed Haj Amin home. Could this red carpet treatment have legitimized the mufti's autocratic approach toward Palestinians? It's worth mulling over. An engineer named Arafat would be learning the "leadership" ropes soon enough. Where did he pick up his tips for rejecting peace with the Jews, waging terror on his own people, and wasting the money intended for their development?

We need honest scrutiny on another post-Holocaust front: why Israel was ultimately born but Palestine was stillborn. In 1947, the United Nations proposed to partition Palestine, envisioning 45 percent of the land for an Arab-governed state, 55 percent for a Jewish state, and a shared Jerusalem to be supervised internationally. Muslims commonly kvetch that the Jews would have gotten more square miles than the Arabs. I think we've gotten our own mileage out of this shallow gripe. Seldom do we admit that the proposed Jewish state, made up mainly of the Negev Desert, would have been etched from the least fertile areas of Palestine. In addition, the proposed Palestinian state would have boasted an overwhelmingly Arab population; not so the Jewish state, which would have had only a thin majority of Jews. However grudgingly, the Jews could live with the "other." They adopted the UN plan and, six months later, proclaimed independence.

Not so the Arabs. They made war against Israel and lost even more territory. Maybe worse for ordinary Palestinians, the various Arab regimes that scooped up their postwar territory only reinforced the prewar democracy deficit. Take it from the eminent scholar Bernard Lewis and his book, *The Middle East: 2000 Years of History from the Rise of Christianity to the Present Day*. "Between 1949 and 1967," he notes, "the Arab League, and in particular the Arab states occupying parts of Palestine, claimed to speak for the Palestinians and discouraged—at times even prevented—any active Palestinian participation in the political process." Again, who's betraying whom?

No, I haven't forgotten about the Cold War. From the late 1940s to the 1960s, superpower strategists transformed the Middle East into a puppet show. To my mind, the most craven example of manipulation came not from the United States, but from the Soviet Union: Joseph Stalin transferred weapons from Czechoslovakia to Israel and helped the Jews withstand their first assault by the Arabs. But shortly after Israel's 1948 victory, Stalin thumbed his nose at Israel, America's ally-to-be, and armed the Arabs. Egypt's Gamal Abdul Nasser was a choice client.

Over the next two decades, Arabs thought they'd found their heir to Saladin, the military commander who deftly repelled Christendom's army during the Crusades for the Holy Land. Deftly, but temporarily. Nasser seized on both legacies. The Egyptian general-turned-president ignited a collective consciousness among Arabs everywhere by standing up to Israel's chief cheerleader, the United States.

Anti-Americanism doesn't equal anticolonialism. Nasser proved as much. Under him, Egypt overdosed on the ideological opiate of the Soviet Union, staking both an economic and a cultural renaissance on socialism. For example, Nasser nationalized Cairo's flagship Al-Azhar University, the Harvard of religious and legal education within Sunni Islam. This attempt to fast-track secularization backfired. "By linking the reformed Azhar institution too directly to the state, Nasser's regime deprived it of credibility," writes Gilles Kepel in *Jihad: The Trail of Political Islam*. "A vacuum had been created, to be filled by anyone ready to question the state and criticize governments in the name of Islam."

The vacuum was about to be filled. Awash in ammunition and pumped with pride, Arabs grew mesmerized by the dream of avenging the Zionist occupation. Instead, a shiny new generation met further dishonor. Israel bested Egypt and its regional allies in the 1967 war. That humiliation translated into the once inconceivable loss of Jerusalem, the unraveling of an identity, and the end of secular socialism as a rallying creed.

Organizing since the 1920s, religious fundamentalists stepped into the breach with bumper-sticker assurances that "Islam is the solution." They didn't lack for listeners or, within a few years, for dollars. The explosion of oil wealth enjoyed by the likes of Saudi Arabia, a country that promulgates a puritan and punitive Islam, spawned funding for the most radical Muslims. "Their great hope," laments Egyptian liberal Gaber Asfour, "has been that a return to strict Islam would provide the strength for a final victory over Zionism and Israel."

We come full circle to Palestine. As strict Islam has gained momentum, Yasser Arafat has customized religious vocabulary and visuals for political ends. In the mid-1970s, he invoked the word "martyr" without any Koranic connotation. Twenty-five years later, not only are young Palestinians immolating themselves and civilians in the name of God, they're also ribbing each other about the limp fate of martyrs in paradise. "In some jokes the black-eyed virgins turn out to be sexless, or the wine is alcohol-free," says Arab Israeli professor Muhammed Abu Samra. These jokes "express a kind of distrust in what the Islamic faith promises in the next life." In the hands of those who use spirituality as a machete, Islam has been no solution at all. Palestinian textbooks, broadcasts, and protests marinate in Muslim zeal. And yet, to quote Abu Samra's summary of street-level sentiment in Palestine, "Everything seems doomed to failure and corruption." Shades of my conversation with the Muslim American woman in the Dome of the Rock.

Two months after that conversation, a former minister in Arafat's cabinet risked his security for his integrity. Nabil Amr wrote an appeal for introspection in one of the Palestinian Authority's official newspapers (a testament to the editor's own backbone in printing it). "We take comfort, Mr. President, in designing excuses," Amr told Arafat. Reminiscent of the ex-guerrillas who wrote an "open manifesto" to the mufti of Jerusalem more than fifty years before, Amr accused the Palestinian chairman of squandering the world's aid and goodwill, as well as a legitimate offer for coexistence with Israel. From an insider's perspective, he exposed the "tribal mind-set" of Palestinian politicians, men robed in the rituals of democracy yet naked egoists underneath. In closing, Amr wrote, "We committed serious mistakes against our people, our Authority, and our dream of statehood. To make up for these mistakes, we must confess our failure first, and then take immediate action. Our people are noble and deserve from us the commitment to think with them and for their benefit. We cannot let our people's destiny be set free to chance, a chance that, under a new world order, may take yet another eternal struggle without opening a door of hope."

Nabil Amr survived the bullets shot at his house by Palestinian hooligans. Since his statement, a few more Palestinians have publicly echoed him. They've acknowledged that Israel is not the alpha and the omega of their people's oppression. So why do we in the West increasingly perceive Israel as *the* viper?

ACTIVISTS FOR PALESTINE ARE RATCHETING UP THE EMOTIONAL tenor of their arguments. Just look at the popularity of comparing Israel to apartheid-era South Africa.

Before my trip to Ramallah, I was searching for information about *Promises,* an Oscar-nominated documentary that profiles Arab and Jewish children living in Jerusalem. Although steeped in antagonistic rhetoric, some of the children change their tune after meeting one another. One Palestinian partisan couldn't abide such affection—or the fact that two of the three filmmakers were American Jews. "[S]econd-generation Zionist propaganda," he fulminated on arabia.com. "Had a documentary been produced in South Africa to gauge the intensity of feelings between Blacks and Whites during Apartheid rule, few people would have described the angry words of Blacks against Whites as a sign of Black racism." As you know, in Ramallah, I'd heard about South Africa again.

After returning to Toronto, I learned that a Palestine solidarity group was sponsoring a South African academic to spread the word on North American campuses that Israel is an apartheid state. Speaking at the University of Toronto—in the Reichmann Family Lecture Hall—the academic drew apartheid-era parallels such as Israel's prohibition on "mixed" marriages. Couples of different faiths, married or not, can live together in Israel. It's the wedding, a religious ceremony, that can't happen within the country. What he didn't mention, I later discovered, is that a Jewish parliamentarian had recently proposed a bill to introduce secular marriages—and that Muslim legislators had allied with Orthodox and ultra-Orthodox Jews to quash the bill.

In a state practicing apartheid, would Arab Muslim legislators wield veto power over anything? At only 20 percent of the population, would Arabs even be eligible for election if they squirmed under the thumb of apartheid? Would an apartheid state extend voting rights to women and the poor in local elections, which Israel did for the first time in the history of Palestinian Arabs? Would the vast majority of Arab Israeli citizens turn out to vote in national elections, as they've usually done? Would an apartheid state have several Arab political parties, as Israel does? Would the judiciary be free of political interference? In the 2003 Israeli elections, two Arab parties found themselves disqualified for expressly supporting terrorism against the Jewish state. Israel's supreme court overturned both disqualifications.

Would an apartheid state award its top literary prize to an Arab? Israel honored Emile Habibi in 1986, before any intifada might have made the choice politically shrewd. Would an apartheid state encourage Hebrew-speaking schoolchildren to learn Arabic? Would road signs throughout the land appear in both languages? (Even the proudly bilingual Canada doesn't meet that standard.) Would an apartheid state be home to universities where Arabs and Jews mingle at will, or apartment blocks where they live side by side? Would an apartheid state bestow benefits and legal protections on Palestinians who live outside of Israel but work inside its borders? Would human rights organizations operate openly in an apartheid state? They do in Israel. For that matter, even military officials go public with their criticisms of government policies. In October 2003, the Israel Defense Forces' Chief of staff told the press that road closures in the West Bank and Gaza were feeding Palestinian anger. Two weeks later, four former heads of the Shin Bet security service blasted the occupation, calling on Ariel Sharon to withdraw troops unilaterally. Would an apartheid state stomach so much dissent from those mandated to defend the state?

Above all, in an apartheid state, would the media debate the moral rectitude of national policies? Would a Hebrew newspaper in an apartheid state run an article by an Arab Israeli about why "the Zionist adventure has been a total failure"? Would it run that article on Israel's own independence day? Would an apartheid state ensure conditions for the freest Arabic press in the Middle East, a press so free that it can demonstrably abuse its liberties and keep on rolling? (To this day, the East Jerusalem daily *Al-Quds* hasn't retracted an anti-Israel letter supposedly penned by Nelson Mandela but proven to have been written by an Arab living in Holland.)

Even the late *éminence grise* of Palestinian nationalism, Edward Said, stated flat out that "Israel is not South Africa . . ." How could it be when an Israeli publisher had translated Said's seminal work, *Orientalism,* into Hebrew? I'll cap this point with a question that Said himself asked of Arabs: "Why don't we fight harder for freedom of opinions in our own societies, a freedom, no one needs to be told, that scarcely exists?"

I disagree—some people still need to be told that Arab "freedoms" don't compare to those of Israel. The people who need reminding are those who now push the South Africa analogy a step further—by equating Israel with Nazi Germany. To them, Zionists are committing hate crimes under the totalitarian nightmare that they dub "Zio-Nazism" (like neo-Nazism).

The sworn enemies of Zio-Nazism made their debut on the international stage in August 2001. At forums leading up to the United Nations World Conference against Racism in Durban, South Africa, the Arab Lawyers Union circulated cartoons depicting vampire-toothed Israeli soldiers with Nazi flags fluttering from their helmets. One such soldier stood sentry at the boarded-up door of a Palestinian office. The boards formed a swastika. Another pro-Palestine leaflet superimposed a swastika on the Star of David. The most malevolent poster distributed at Durban featured Hitler speculating, "What If I Had Won?" Under the heading "Good Things," this poster had the führer saying, "There would be NO Israel and NO Palestinian's blood shed. The rest is your guess."

How, though, can one claim to be fighting Nazism while making common cause with Hitler? The answer is your guess.

I'm revolted by how much more inspiration from Hitler these tacticians take. It's no coincidence that in the cartoons circulated at Durban, Israeli soldiers had dripping fangs. Too many Arab Muslim intellectuals, journalists, and politicians tell their audiences that Jews are Nazis because they siphon the blood of non-Jewish children for religious observances. Known as the blood libel, this fiction was itself a favorite calumny against Jews in the Nazi publication *Der Stürmer.* In this way, too, some maligners of Israel hop into bed with Hitler. They copy the Nazis in order to oppose what they call Nazism. I just don't get it.

And their illogic is being indulged at the highest diplomatic echelons. No less a figure than the Syrian defense minister is publishing books and producing a movie to tag Jews as bloodsuckers. Not metaphorical bloodsuckers, mind you—literal bloodsuckers. Yet, far from having to explain itself at the United Nations World Conference against Racism, Syria sat on the UN human rights commission from 2001 to 2003. That's in addition to being made a rotating member of the prestigious UN Security Council. Ready for the coup de grâce? Israel was the only country in the world to be criticized in documents presented at the official UN conference against racism. Why this staggering moral disconnect?

Somebody?

At the end of the day, I believe it's about how you define Zionism. To its proponents, Zionism represents the homecoming of a historically persecuted and demographically dwindling people. But to its opponents, Zionism is racism—an ideology incubated by wealthy European Jews who capitalized on the assumption that God's "chosen people" can steal land and populate it through a discriminatory Law of Return. The law applies to those who share one exclusive and exclusionary trait: Jewish lineage. Just as the Third Reich lionized the racial purity of Aryans, so Israel exists to nourish the biological privilege of Jews.

Let's figure out what's what. David Matas, the well-known international human rights lawyer, suggests it's bizarre to conflate Zionism and racism. "Jews come in every color," he reminds us. "There are black Jews—Falashas—who, under the Law of Return, were airlifted from Ethiopia to Israel." Which jolts me into thinking that if pro-Palestine activists cared to be remotely accurate rather than ardent, their cartoons would demonize brown Israeli soldiers. And black ones. Why is it that the villains are all white, all the time? My question leads to the bigger one posed by Matas: Can the Law of Return, which encompasses every race, be legitimately stamped "racist"? Fair point. But I'm also aware that in Israel an eighteen-year-old Ethiopian Jewish soldier can request the identity card of a sixty-year-old Arab. The Arab and his family have harvested the Holy Land for generations and must now cower before a kid who's been in Israel for eight months. I can see why the Arab feels humiliated. His, too, is a fair point. Where does that leave us?

When it comes to citizenship, Israel does discriminate. In the way that an affirmative action policy discriminates, Israel gives the edge to a specific minority that has faced historical injustice. In that sense, the Jewish state is an affirmative action polity. Liberals should love it.

Does Israel's affirmative action amount to Nazism? Spare me. As a Muslim, I could become a citizen of Israel without having to convert; it would happen under the naturalization process rather than the Law of Return, but it would happen. After all, Israel was one of the few countries anywhere to grant shelter, then citizenship, to the Vietnamese boat people who sought political asylum in the late 1970s. I don't have to wonder how Syria compares on that score. Now for the ultimate proof of Israel's flimsy credentials as a bunker of Hitlerian hate: It's the only country in the Middle East to which Arab Christians are voluntarily migrating. They're also thriving, notching much higher university attendance rates than the Arab Muslim citizens of Israel and enjoying better overall health than Jews themselves.

The twice-promised land is gut-wrenching and complicated. Israeli Jews have their struggles with each other, to say nothing of the daily tangle with Arabs. There's little point in deciding who's the paragon of vice or virtue. The better question might be this: Who's willing to hear what they don't want to hear? Israel, I find, brings more compassion to "colonization" than its adversaries have ever brought to "liberation." The Jewish state negotiates tensions openly. That's the stuff of genuine democracy. Can meaningful democracy be seen in any Islamic state today?

IF ISRAELI IMPERIALISM ISN'T THE CORK IN THE BOTTLE THAT contains our democratic genie, you might want to tell me that the United States is. Forget the woolly-headed Islamists; countless reform-minded Muslims call America "the problem." It's a soothing conclusion to reach, what with U.S. power being pilloried from various directions. But beneath all the sneering and sloganeering lurks Muslim admiration . . . for America.

Let me take you back to Israel for a moment. Bounding through the market in the Muslim quarter of Jerusalem, I happened upon a surreal sight. Above my head, in Halloween black and orange, two signs advertised the Holy Rock Café. Its logo left no doubt what reputation the Holy Rock was supposed to summon, that of the Hard Rock Café. Neither a franchise nor a knockoff, this unkempt, unadorned eatery nonetheless took its cue from America. Something tells me the CIA didn't make the restaurant do it.

Thomas Friedman, foreign affairs columnist for the *New York Times,* had a similar experience in Doha, Qatar. Strolling through what he hoped was an authentic Qatari tableau, he "rounded one corner and suddenly it appeared before me, like a huge blot on the horizon: Taco Bell." Even more unsettling, he stresses, *It was crowded!"*

Notice where I'm heading? When Muslims blast U.S. imperialism, God knows we're not always talking cultural imperialism.

Fact is, if given the choice to embrace or erase Western popular culture, most Muslims gleefully embrace it. Those who can afford it enroll their children in North American and European schools. One columnist minced no words about this in the Pakistani weekly, *DAWN:* "Listen to a Muslim intellectual, mullah, or politician and you will hear a litany of complaints and criticism against Western sins of omission and commission. . . . Ask him where he wants to send his children to university and, if he is honest, he will reel off the names of the top American universities. And if he is well placed in his own country, he will move heaven and earth to try and get the American mission to intercede to get his child a college place or a student visa. Indeed, he will perjure himself to get financial assistance for his offspring by declaring his insolvency." Down with America— but not till my kid graduates.

Then there are experiences beyond education. Far more Muslim families vacation in the West than in the Islamic world. Al-Jazeera TV runs American ads for perfumes and buys programming from American archives. On Al-Jazeera's rival network, the Middle East Broadcasting Centre, *Who Wants to Be a Millionaire* has smashed ratings records. In pre-Internet days, journalists in the region clamored to read Western newspapers for an insight into independent reporting. They coveted jobs that exposed them to professional standards. More telling, Pepsi cans litter the path to the Cave of Hirah, where Prophet Muhammad reputedly imbibed the words of God.

Nora Kevorkian, a friend who made the documentary *Veils Uncovered,* has this on videotape: In a Damascus market, black-draped women purchase lingerie that smacks of American raunch. One pair of electric panties features an illuminated Tweety Bird that sings. Another has Bugs Bunny beckoning us to "Kiss me." A third pair chimes, "We Wish You a Merry Christmas," batteries not included. "Everyone buys," the merchant says gleefully about these items. Who wants to be a millionaire? He does.

Such is the Muslim adoration for Western culture that it has generated buzz about a Jewish conspiracy. Recently, mullahs in myriad patches of the Middle East denounced Pokémon (the children's video game) as a Japanese word that translates into "I am Jewish." A Saudi cleric attributed the "Pokémon craze" to "a Jewish plot aimed at forcing our children to forgo their faith and values and distract them from more important things such as scientific ambitions." The little icons of licentiousness—and I'm not referring to the mullahs—got slapped with a fatwa.

It's time to bring out the deeper point. The fact that so many Muslims covet the American way of life holds the key to why they're also furious with Washington. It's not jealousy so much as unrequited camaraderie. For all the goods and services that America markets to Muslim societies, the greatest good, the greatest service—freedom—remains underpromoted. Some Americans will scratch their heads at this, baffled as to why they don't get credit for liberating Kuwait and protecting Saudi Arabia from Saddam Hussein's chemical-tipped claws in 1991. It's because most Arabs believe the U.S. rescued the royal families, not the people—"a big difference," writes Fareed Zakaria, editor of *Newsweek International*. "Even in the rich Gulf states one senses the frustration and anger of a populace that has been given some wealth but no voice—locked in a gilded cage."

And sometimes, not so gilded. "It bothers me to see the world live in freedom, something we don't have," sighs a captive housewife in *Veils Uncovered*. "Why is our life so different from theirs?" She nervously though resolutely removes her cloak for the camera. "It is important that the world see how we live our life."

Her country, Syria, does business with the United States—the nasty business that other Muslim states do. Washington contracts them to torture political detainees who are suspected of being terrorists. That way, America can claim a relatively stainless record on human rights. Problem is, easily caught in the same net with those tortured by Syria and company are human rights activists. No shocker there: To the authoritarian regimes with which America allies itself, human rights advocates *are* enemies. Why doesn't America roar in defense of these lonely voices, who often risk life and limb to introduce the democratic ideals that Washington insists are imperative? Reform-loving Muslims have to wonder: Is America with us—or with the autocrats?

President George W. Bush tackled that question in June 2002. "In our development aid, in our diplomatic efforts, in our international broadcasting, and in our educational assistance, the United States will promote moderation and human rights," he told the graduating class of West Point Military Academy. The following month, his sincerity would face a test emanating from one of Washington's biggest client states, Egypt.

IN JULY 2002, SAAD EDDIN IBRAHIM ENTERED A JAIL CELL FOR THE second time in as many years. His sentence of seven years with the possibility of hard labor "is almost like a death certificate" for civil liberties in Egypt, said the publisher of the *Cairo Times*. What exactly landed the sixty-five-year-old sociology professor in prison remains murky. He'd long been a friend to Egyptian president Hosni Mubarak, overseeing Mrs. Mubarak's master's thesis and writing speeches for her. Ibrahim hosted a weekly TV show about social development, conducted seminal research into the motives of Muslim militants, and represented Egypt at international conferences on human rights. But all of that preceded June 30, 2000—the night of his first arrest. Over the next twenty-four months of lengthy detentions, show trials, and prison stints, it became obvious to him that "those I had angered decided to act to eliminate Saad Eddin Ibrahim from Egypt's public life."

His opponents' sulfurous anger had likely been bubbling since the mid-1990s. As head of the Ibn Khaldun Center for Development Studies in Cairo, Ibrahim felt a duty to imbue his work with the spirit of the center's namesake. Among the last towering intellects of Islam's golden age, Ibn Khaldun turned history and sociology into respectable disciplines. On the shoulders of this pioneer, Ibrahim broke new ground—at least for the Arab Muslim world—in 1994. He organized a conference about minority rights. At the time, Egypt clung to a law that required Coptic Christians to secure the president's approval before repairing their churches. Puncturing Egypt's official line that Muslims live in seamless harmony with Christians, Ibrahim deemed the Copts a minority that suffers government persecution. Strike One. A year later, he and other democracy advocates monitored Egypt's parliamentary elections. They exposed a level of fraud previously unthinkable, given the country's image as an oasis of Arab enlightenment. Strike Two. Ibrahim's findings foreshadowed the direction in which Egypt was not just drifting, but hurtling: corrupt despotism in place of an already frail democracy.

I don't want to be naive about democracy. I know that Egypt had to get tough after Muslim fanatics assassinated President Anwar Sadat in 1981. That's when Egypt adopted the Emergency Law, under which thousands of Islamists have been jailed for two decades now. And many pose an unmistakable threat: One Sabbath afternoon in 1994, Egypt's Nobel Prize–winning

novelist, Naguib Mafouz, settled into a car. Young religious ruf-
fians took advantage of the open window and plunged a kitchen
knife into Mafouz's neck. The eighty-two-year-old was lucky
to emerge with only a paralyzed arm. (What a thing to "only"
suffer.) Reports later surfaced that Mafouz's would-be murderers stalked him because of a book he'd written three decades
earlier. Its characters reminded some readers of Islamic historical figures. The attackers turned allegory into reality and pun-
ished Mafouz for their interpretation of his work. Excuse me,
but if that's a reason to maim (and potentially kill), it's equally a
reason for security forces to crack down on the thugs. Bring on
the Emergency Law.

What Ibrahim spotlighted is the way this Emergency Law has
been exploited for corrupt ends. The Egyptian government plays
into clerical heavy-handedness so that conservative Muslims can
be appeased. As a result, the state zaps religious modernizers
along with militants.

There's the absurd case of Cairo University professor Nasr
Hamed Abu-Zeid. He wrote a book arguing that the meaning
of scripture can become "more humanistic" even as the verses
remain unchanged. He submitted this book to an academic
committee reviewing his application for a promotion. The
unsuspecting professor soon faced the charge of "apostate."
Islamist lawyers took him to court, demanding that the infidel
divorce his wife. In 1995, the Islamists won. Egypt's justice minister has the power to overturn such a verdict and, so far, hasn't.
The hounded couple now lives in Holland, from the safety of
which Abu-Zeid is countersuing the Egyptian justice minister.

Throughout it all, Saad Ibrahim has been asserting a crucial
connection: "Societies that restrict the space for citizens to participate and express dissent will eventually spawn a twisted,

angry, and lethal response." In other words, Islamists gain blood-thirsty adherents when fair political representation no longer exists. And it doesn't exist, Ibrahim pointed out. While clamping down on liberal Muslims might give conservatives the mirage of being heard, a mirage is all it is, because legitimate avenues of representation, such as legislatures, are shrinking into fiefdoms of the government's friends. Five years after Ibrahim sounded the siren of a diminishing democracy, the *Washington Quarterly* printed this observation about Egypt: "In a country that mandates that fully half the members of parliament must be either peasants or laborers, the current configuration is solidly tilted toward a tiny elite." That was in 2000.

The year 2000 proved utterly kooky, both for Ibrahim and for the state of Egyptian democracy. He had just returned home from Washington, where a human rights watchdog celebrated his commitment to freedom, when violence erupted between Muslims and Coptic Christians in Upper Egypt. Some two dozen people died, many more were injured, and a hundred shops and homes were looted. Of the previous fifty-five sectarian clashes over thirty years, Ibrahim judged this one to be "the ugliest and largest." So he pulled together five hundred public figures to sign a proclamation, coupled with policy suggestions, to end "an emerging pattern of sectarian strife." According to Ibrahim, the Mubarak government took this gesture as "an outright defiance. Publicizing the seriousness of the sectarian problem was considered as tarnishing the wholly perfect and tolerant face of Egypt, a crime punishable—we soon learned—under a law from the 1920s, never used to prosecute [an] Egyptian citizen before."

Ibrahim wouldn't be arrested for several months yet. Meanwhile, he and his colleagues at the Ibn Khaldun Center kept busy training students to record human rights violations and monitor elections. In preparation for the nationwide vote, the professor teamed up with another firecracker, playwright Ali Salem, to produce a video about why Egyptians should bother to cast ballots. (If anybody could make civic education entertaining, it's the wickedly populist Salem. One of his books, *A Drive to Israel,* captured the humanity of the Jewish state and got Salem thrown out of the Arab Writers' Union. Among Egyptians, *A Drive to Israel* was a best-seller.) Somewhere along the way, Ibrahim also gave an interview in which he implied that Egypt might be oxidizing into just another Arab family dynasty. Strikes Three, Four, and Five.

On the evening of June 30, 2000, officers rounded up Ibrahim and twenty-seven others from the Ibn Khaldun Center as well as the League of Egyptian Women Voters. A forty-five-day detention led to a seven-month trial in State Security Court, a military-style tribunal that operates outside the rules of due process. Government prosecutors scrambled for a case. First, they accused Ibrahim of misusing money that he received from the European Union for his get-out-the-vote video. But the EU declared Ibrahim squeaky clean. Next, prosecutors argued that he shouldn't have accepted outside funds—a "laughable" suggestion, clucked one Arab journalist, considering that the Egyptian government survives on foreign aid. Regardless, the court convicted all twenty-eight defendants. Ibrahim got seven years.

Ten months into the sentence, during which he suffered a series of minor strokes, Ibrahim received word that a retrial would be granted. Might justice prevail after all? Judge for yourself. As the second trial got under way in the summer of 2002, Egypt's parliamentarians rammed through a law severely restricting the work of nongovernmental groups. Back in court, the grab bag of charges against Ibrahim and his codefendants seemed to hinge on one accusation—that they, and especially he as their ringleader, had "defamed" Egypt's reputation abroad. The trial concluded in July 2002, with prison terms for five of the twenty-eight defendants. Again, Ibrahim was condemned to seven years. The official reason: his decade-old statement that the government represses Egypt's Christians.

If only as a faith-based initiative, President Bush ought to have publicly protested and put the squeeze on Mubarak. Egypt's religious minorities need an indefatigable champion like Ibrahim. But beyond that, Ibrahim presented the perfect test of Bush's stated foreign policy goals: moderation and human rights. For one thing, his health—already marred by heart trouble—was sure to worsen in prison. Moreover, Ibrahim has an American wife and is a naturalized U.S. citizen; protecting their citizens from harm is what American presidents do, no? Finally, under the peace accord with Israel, Egypt benefits from nearly $2 billion in U.S. aid every year. That's 10 percent of America's entire foreign aid budget. On this basis alone, one of Washington's most conservative publications encouraged Bush to exercise America's "abundant leverage with Egypt" and secure clemency for Ibrahim. He could have gone much further than he did.

Here's how far Bush did venture: In August 2002, he suspended a $130 million planned hike in aid to Egypt. With word of his decision, the president included a letter of concern about Ibrahim's conviction. That's not peanuts. In Egypt, bureaucrats and intellectuals went berserk over Bush's intervention. A hundred Arabs from around the world nonetheless followed Bush's lead and sent Mubarak their own letter to support Ibrahim. A few months later, the Egyptian government announced Ibrahim's eligibility for a third trial and released him until then. In March 2003, the trial cleared Ibrahim once and for all. Directly or obliquely, Bush got results by leaning on Mubarak, and we should credit the U.S. president for applying one of his favorite axioms: When you have political capital, use it or lose it.

Why, then, didn't Bush openly push for Ibrahim's pardon, thereby putting his ally—and the entire Islamic world—on notice that democracy is no crime? One word, according to the critics: Iraq. War clouds were gathering against Iraq and America had to charm Egypt to come onside. Perhaps unfairly, many Muslims scoff that Bush will do the military hustle for democracy in Iraq but won't fully flex his diplomatic muscle for democracy in Egypt. Other than that, Mr. President, we enjoyed your speech to the 2002 West Point graduates.

WHICH BRINGS ME BACK TO MY POINT: AMERICA ISN'T LOATHED by Muslims so much as it's loved—loved to the point of being needed. More proof came in the spring of 2003.

When Saddam's statue ate dust, raw jubilation swirled up in Baghdad. In the days after, I went to a victory party in Toronto organized by young, mostly secular, Muslims. A group of them buttonholed me to say they found it strange that more Muslims weren't admitting the wisdom of a preemptive strike against Saddam. Strange, they said, because preemptive action was exactly the strategy used by Prophet Muhammad to oust those whom he suspected of plotting against Islam. "If preemptive war was good for Muslims then," shrugged one of the celebrants, "why not for Americans now?"

"Because standards of behavior have evolved since the seventh century," I said, playing the contrarian.

"Tell that to the Islamic countries that still treat women like dirt."

"And make life hell for religious minorities," I added. Others jumped in. We expressed disgust that Muslim "antiwar" activists remained tight-lipped about the war against all sorts of people being carried out in Allah's name. As we swapped observations, it became clear to us that Muslims have a choice to make: Acknowledge that Prophet Muhammad's preemptive assaults on Jews were morally wrong, in which case Muslims have credibility when slamming the Bush doctrine, or accept what the Prophet did as necessary and divinely guided, in which case the same could be said for Bush, a born-again Christian who has his own communion with God. Muslims can't have it both ways. That's called a double standard. Isn't it only Americans who practice that?

There will always be a contingent of anti-Americans and isolationists, Muslim and not, who want Washington to butt out. However, many young Muslims I talked to even before this party want Washington to "butt in"—and follow through—on behalf of human rights.

IF THEY COULD SAY SO WITHOUT BEING OSTRACIZED, THEY'D URGE America to brandish its influence and help change these realities:

- In Tunisia and Algeria, Muslim women can't legally marry outside the faith. Men, on the other hand, can. In most Muslim countries, marital rape, if recognized at all, isn't considered a crime.
- Saudi Arabia recently arrested a ninety-four-year-old man, laying claim to the world's oldest known political prisoner, though he was released two weeks later. Sheikh Mohamed Ali al-Amri, a prominent Shia cleric in Medina, inflamed

Saudi authorities by receiving several Shia visitors at his farm. They'd come to pray. Like the Copts in Egypt, Shia Muslims in Saudi Arabia are legally suppressed.

· A majority of the world's refugees spill out from Islamic countries. Not surprising, since most of the world's civil wars rage among Muslims. Says Iranian journalist Amir Taheri, "The Arab states have fought no fewer than fifteen open or secret wars against one another since the 1930s . . ." In the past ten years, Islamists and their socialist foes have butchered a hundred thousand Algerians. In February 1982, the Baathist forces of Syria's Hafez Assad bombarded a town harboring Muslim extremists. His hoodlums obliterated 25,000 people. And from 1975 to 1990, the Lebanese civil war cost at least 150,000 lives, most of them belonging to Palestinians. That's more than ten times as many deaths as Israel has inflicted in fifty years of combat.

If any of this is embarrassing to admit, my fellow Muslims, get over it. Because we know that we can't pin our basest ills on America. The cancer begins with us. In a moving column about Muslim "wretchedness" published shortly after September 11 in *The Nation*, a Pakistani daily, businessman Izzat Majeed spoke of "an increasing awareness" among Muslims "that we have failed as a civil society by not confronting the historical, social and political demons within us." Like the fact that, in his country of 140 million, only 1 million tax returns are filed annually. By abdicating their responsibility to give something back, aren't the tax evaders prodding Pakistan's government into near-bankruptcy, starving public programs such as education, and feeding the demand for those terror tutorials that so many madressas have become?

Are most of us conscious of what this multicultural Muslim nation was intended to be? I'll fill you in. The year was 1947. In his first speech as the governor-general of independent Pakistan, Muhammad Ali Jinnah exuded high hopes for the people. "You are free," he gushed. "You are free to go to your temples, you are free to go to your mosques, or to any other place of worship in the State of Pakistan. You may belong to any religion or caste or creed—that has nothing to do with the business of the state. We are starting with this fundamental principle that we are all citizens of one state. . . . You will find that in due course of time, Hindus will cease to be Hindus and Muslims will cease to be Muslims, not in the religious sense . . . but in the political sense as citizens of the state." Jinnah had a non-Muslim wife whom he adored. His sister, Fatima, frequently appeared with him in the campaign to create Pakistan. Her visibility reopened the Muslim imagination to the potential of women as partners rather than handmaidens. I'm no fan of the fact that Muslims demanded a state separate from India, but when they got it, at least it came with the premise and promise of individual freedoms.

A shame about the demise of Pakistan under the rising tide of Islamism, don't you think? In 1977, a U.S.-backed military coup installed General Zia al-Haq, who loved golf, tennis, and absolute order. To cement his tenuous grip, the strongman surrounded himself with sycophantic mullahs who referred to him as "Commander of the Faithful," a term reserved for Prophet Muhammad's successors. To curry favor among village leaders, Zia mixed a punitive reading of Islam with tribal customs. In this way, stoning arose as a legal punishment for adultery, and it was required that a rape be witnessed by four men before any offender could be charged. But suppose a rape doesn't have the testimony of so many male eyes? Then it must naturally be a case of adultery, committed by the woman, and therefore to be condemned by the stone.

In 1979, at about the same time as these laws began their chokehold, Pakistan's Abdus Salam shared the Nobel Prize in physics with two Americans. You'd think Salam's country would have feted him. Instead, rioters tried to prevent him from reentering Pakistan. An act of parliament even took away his citizenship. Salam's crime? He was an Ahmadi—a minority sect within Islam. That's it. That's what made an internationally acclaimed Muslim scientist persona non grata in his own homeland.

I picked up other details about Abdus Salam from a Toronto cabdriver named Ahmed. Trusting me as that "Muslim on TV," he bemoaned "how our people are killing each other," focusing more on "tribe" than on "love." Love! I'd never heard a Muslim man use the L-word. This guy had to be different, so I probed. Turns out that the cabbie himself was an Ahmadi. I asked him about Abdus Salam on the off chance that he'd know the name. In the rearview mirror, I watched Ahmed's eyebrows lift. "Brother Abdus tried to donate his [Nobel] Prize money to the government," he told me. "He wanted science labs to be built for young Pakistanis. But Zia rejected his offer." Ahmed confided a second reason for considering Abdus Salam his hero: As the son of a farmer, Salam had no dearth of odds to overcome. Apparently, he worked so hard at learning that, in the absence of oil for the kerosene lanterns at school, he studied under street lamps. True or not, this narrative could have fueled one hell of a national myth to inspire generations of humble Pakistanis to greatness. Instead, the government trashed Abdus Salam—and loads more intellectual capital—in rabid pursuit of a narrow Islam.

Zia's prejudices live on despite his death in 1988. Since then, Islamism has gained momentum thanks in large measure to filthy geopolitics. In 1989, thousands of *mujahideen,* or holy warriors, beat back the Soviet invasion of Afghanistan. As Arab Muslim soldiers came home to the Persian Gulf, American troops arrived in Saudi Arabia to protect it from a potential Iraqi incursion. In 1990, you'll recall, Saddam Hussein invaded and occupied Kuwait. The Saudis feared he'd try the same with them. Wanting to take no chances, they asked Americans to defend their soil—and their oil. America's presence in Saudi Arabia could have been the excuse for out-of-work mujahideen to mount a jihad within the kingdom. But a king's ransom was paid to avoid it. Petrodollars coursed through Islamic charities and drove the exponential growth of madressas across the region. Pakistan wound up with a huge cut of the funds, and its madressas soon churned out elite Taliban alumni. What did middle-class Muslims in Pakistan do? Most allowed themselves to go with the flow of brutal fundamentalism.

One voice of dissent was that of Pakistani diplomat and scholar Akbar Ahmed. In 1997, he started filming an epic biography of Jinnah, Pakistan's founding father. According to Ahmed, "important officials" and "concerned citizens" in Pakistan warned him not to depict Jinnah's tolerant Islam. Newspapers and political parties even hallucinated that "Salman Rushdie had written the script." To top it off, they regarded his project "part of a Hindu or a Zionist conspiracy." Ahmed made the movie anyway and won several international awards. But, as with Abdus Salam, the accolades from home would be measly.

Since September 11, Pakistani leader Pervez Musharraf has steeled his spine and stated the obvious: Muslims today "are the poorest, the most illiterate, the most backward, the most unhealthy, the most unenlightened, the most deprived, and the weakest of all the human race." Fine words coming from a man who reneged on promises to curb the blasphemy laws and regulate the madressas. What Musharraf doesn't dare say is that his country's mullah-mauled schools continue breeding imbeciles. Akbar Ahmed can tell you. On a recent trip back to Pakistan, he approached madressa teachers about the need to study Sigmund Freud and Max Weber. "I was met with an uncomprehending stare. I realized the depth of the problem when I even received a negative response to my suggestion that Muslim scholars such as historian Ibn Khaldun or mystic poet Mowlana Rumi be taught." This isn't the West keeping Muslims in the dark about our potential for creative excellence. The culprits are Muslims themselves.

By the same token, most Americans need to learn that they have an enlightened self-interest in "being there" for democracy-minded Muslims before the next crisis breaks out. Consider how American attention could have spared millions of innocents the wrath of the Taliban, never mind Al-Qaeda. We've all heard that President Ronald Reagan lavished praise and weapons on the mujahideen as part of his strategy to fight communism. But he gave them more. The U.S. government also funded violence-strewn textbooks published by the University of Nebraska. Where American kids might have subtracted apples from oranges, Afghan students picked up math—and doctrine—from pages filled with pictures of bayonets. Some students still do: The textbooks are only slowly disappearing from Afghan schools.

It doesn't take a four-star general to discern the lesson here. When the Soviets pulled out of Afghanistan in 1989, the United States walked away from a mission presumably accomplished. What it really walked away from was a power struggle. Being seasoned warriors, the mujahideen organized a coup in Afghanistan over the next several years. Even so, A-list Americans didn't much care. In 1998, a Paris publication interviewed Zbigniew Brzezinski, who had been President Jimmy Carter's national security advisor. Now that "Islamic fundamentalism represents a world menace," asked *Le Nouvel Observateur,* should U.S. foreign policy have paid it more heed? Brzezinski, who owed no fealty to the Reagan or Clinton administrations, replied with prickly shortsightedness: "What is most important to the history of the world? Some stirred-up Muslims or the liberation of Central Europe and the end of the Cold War?"

He would have been smarter to recall the odor that President Dwight D. Eisenhower smelled in the late 1950s. During a staff discussion, Eisenhower noted a "campaign of hatred against us not by the governments but by the people" of the Arab world. His National Security Council analyzed the situation and reached a conclusion: Ordinary Arabs felt that by supporting oppressive regimes for the sake of controlling oil flows, the U.S. was blocking democracy. That insight had been on the radar for forty years by the time the Taliban took over Afghanistan and provided safe haven to Al-Qaeda terrorists. Forty years, and it still hadn't registered.

I wish I could say Washington's myopia has been as chastened as the former regimes of Afghanistan and Iraq. I can't. Allow me to illustrate with a conversation I recently watched between talk-show host Phil Donahue and Chuck Dolan, then the vice-chairman of the U.S. Advisory Commission on Public Diplomacy—a body that tries to counter negative impressions of America around the world.

DOLAN: "I think the Bush administration has done some brilliant things since they've been in office in terms of public diplomacy. The jury's still out on some of them, but they're trying—"

DONAHUE: "Abandoning Kyoto [the environmental protocol], not wanting to have anything to do with the International Criminal Court, bad-mouthing the United Nations. We do look like we just want to ride into town all by ourselves, we don't need anybody helpin' us.'"

DOLAN: "Phil, if you want me to talk about their policies, we can do another five shows."

DONAHUE: "But we're talking about why we should be perceived this way! It looks like we don't want to play with anybody else, any kind of international organization! We look arrogant in this posture."

[*silence*]

DOLAN: "But I'm talking about the way we communicate with the world—what we were just talking about. How do we respond to false images of the U.S. abroad? I think that's what we're talking about."

Was Dolan daft? I acknowledge that he couldn't slag his boss or his policies on camera, but that's hardly the point. Dolan didn't want to go near questions about whether these are, in fact, false images of America. He only wanted to talk about how to combat such images with communications tools and tactics. Surprise! Dolan is also a senior vice-president at Ketchum, a PR agency. Come on, America, that's not the essence of public diplomacy. A genuine effort to *do* right, rather than *look* right, ought to be the order of the day.

America, your thrashing of the Taliban made millions of Afghans happy. Since then, though, your failure to post soldiers beyond Kabul has made only tribal warlords and Taliban sympathizers smile. To be sure, a new constitution introduces women's rights and independent courts. On paper. In reality, a warlord whom the U.S. Secretary of Defense recently described as "an appealing person, thoughtful and measured" has brought back the Department of Vice and Virtue. This department enforces strict segregation between girls and boys, mocks freedom of the press, bans poetry readings, beats women who have the tenacity to start their own associations, and tills the soil for the Taliban to return. Thoughtful? Measured? America, are you serious? If so, where are you outside of Kabul? You don't like the idea of your soldiers as peacekeepers, but in that case, why not accelerate your training of local police and beef up the international forces already there? What happened to your instinct for security—and for freedom?

As for you, my fellow Muslims, I hear your resentment. Washington has to appreciate that when liberal Muslims snarl, "We hate you," it's less because America is directly brutalizing the Islamic world than because America is failing, against its own security interests, to help alleviate the brutality for the long term. "Wise up!" you want to yell at Washington. I do, too. But to you, I want to yell, "Grow up!" Liberal Muslims have to get vocal about this fact: Washington is the unrealized hope, not the lead criminal. That President Bush went to bat for Saad Ibrahim, and consequently for Egyptian democracy, gives us reason to have faith in America. I ask of you what Ibrahim asked of his nation's voters: Park the cynicism and be constructive. It's possible that Americans need *our* help to grasp their glorious potential as humanitarians.

TO GET THERE, MUSLIMS HAVE TO TAKE UP A BASIC QUESTION: Precisely what do we need help to reform? What exactly is the private problem that has ballooned to become everybody else's? Since neither Israel nor America lies at the root of Muslim mis-ery worldwide, is it Islam that does? Islam binds the panorama of cultures from North Africa to South Asia, and in each of these cultures, economies and human rights records lag behind most of the globe. Is Islam the *über*-oppressor of creativity, dynamism, and democracy?

It would be too easy to just say no. Think about it this way: The Muslim state of Pakistan was born in 1947, one year before the Jewish state of Israel. Had Jinnah's vision prevailed, Pakistan could have been as modern, as pluralistic, and yet as spiritual as Israel. It turned out just the opposite: more feudal than modern, more sectarian than pluralistic, more maniacal than spiritual. Let me push the comparison. In 2002, a doubles tennis team consisting of a Pakistani and an Israeli made headlines on the circuit. They hit the news not just because they represented the prospect of cooperation between Muslims and Jews, but also because of the reactions from their respective countries. The Israel Tennis Association approved of their man. The Pakistan Tennis Association threatened their guy with a ban. When Israel can see beyond politics despite being under daily siege from its Muslim neighbors, why can't—or won't—Pakistan rise to the challenge? Surely this dichotomy has something to do with each nation's ethical compass, animated as it must be by each nation's religious values. And surely the fact that democracy survives in Israel says something about the popular practice of Judaism that can't be said for mainstream Islam—at least not yet.

But none of this *has* to mean that Islam is the problem. After all, most of the world's Muslims—that is, Muslims outside of the Middle East—live in electoral democracies. At the same time, though, their governments offer few freedoms and little accountability. Maybe Islam's potential for meaningful democracy shines through in the fact that the Koran doesn't prescribe any specific form of government. Assuming the Koran is the work of God—in whole or in part—wouldn't this silence be deliberate? Wouldn't it connote that we, as individuals endowed with free will, ought to participate in our governance? That makes sense if Muslims are a community brought together by faith in God. Everyone says we are. We believe we are. We must be.

Suppose we're not. Suppose we're not really joined by faith in God but by submission to a particular culture. Could it be that Islam, even of the passive sort, is more a faith in the ways of the desert than in the wisdom of the divine, and that Muslims are taught to imitate the power dynamics of an Arabian tribe, where sheikhs rule the roost and everyone else chafes under their rule? Listen closely to Saudi Arabia's King Fahd. The "democratic system prevalent in the world is not appropriate in this region," he says. "The election system has no place in the Islamic creed" since Islam views the leader as a "shepherd" who's responsible for "his flock." Not only does the king equate Muslims with sheep, but he seamlessly suggests that what's bad for desert Arabia—the "region"—must be bad for Islam—the "creed." You might protest, along with me, that he's wrong to make that leap. Clearly, though, Muslims aren't protesting it en masse. We should, not least because the Saudi monarch bears the title Custodian of the Two Holy Shrines—the Prophet's mosques in Mecca and Medina. Who elected him to be Islam's steward? We didn't. Who humors him? We do. But we pay a serious price for not even thinking about it.

Is colonization by desert Arabia *the* problem that we need help to reform?

6

THE HIDDEN
UNDERBELLY OF ISLAM

Not long ago, during coming-out week at a North American
university, I addressed the topic of God and gays. Mine was an
ecumenical perspective, starting with Christianity and building
toward Judaism and Islam. People of these three religions, all
three religions, and of no religion, packed the lecture hall. Only
one cluster came organized. The Muslim Students Association
sent a battalion of members to line the perimeter of the room.
They all remained standing, so that whenever I'd look up from
my notes, whatever direction I'd be facing, I wouldn't fail to see
the unamused, authentic visage of Islam.

In the question and answer session, I lobbed a query to my
audience. If Islam is the "straight path," then why are there
detours in practice? Why can my friend from the Middle East
call Islam a progressive force, citing the opportunity to design
her own hijab, while another friend mails me a postcard from
Pakistan showing women who are body-bagged with barely
a slit for seeing or breathing? ("Greetings from Peshawar!"

exulted the Taliban-era postcard.) My intent was to suggest that Islam isn't as explicit on all matters as Muslims tend to be told.

That point got lost in the ensuing uproar. "Why the difference in practice?" shouted a member of the Muslim Students Association from the back of the room. "Because Pakistanis are not real Muslims. They're converts. Islam was revealed to the Arabs." At this, his South Asian cohorts spun their heads away from me and toward him in horror and hurt. The antiqueer brigade of the Muslim Students Association fell apart before my eyes.

The next day, a Pakistani woman e-mailed me. She wanted to apologize for being one of the students who tried to stare me down. No harm done, I said. Harm had been done, she replied. Stung by her Arab colleague's implication that she was only a Muslim wannabe, she had spent the night reflecting. "I reserve the right to challenge gays," she emphasized, "but I have to say that I wasn't comfortable doing it by trying to unnerve you. In my gut, I know argument deserves counter-argument. I just didn't know how to dissent with 'central command.'" In subsequent e-mails, she clarified that she meant *Arab* central command. She also wondered if the Arab racism within her club would be dealt with.

I wondered the same thing throughout my years at *Queer-Television*. An inordinate number of Muslim viewers tore into my spiritual credentials on purely ethnic grounds. My favorite letter from a "proud Arab" baptized me as a "lying, pig dyke" because an "Indian peasant" such as myself would have no understanding of Islam. Mercy. Little did he understand that my life as an adolescent felt so Arabized that when kids would label me a "Paki," I fought back by telling them I was actually an Arab. To the *QueerTelevision* viewer who dubbed me a pig, I simply responded that we Muslims aren't allowed to eat pigs; does it make any sense that we can *be* pigs? The only thing he needed to get "straight" was his slurs.

At the time, I didn't clue in to the larger point. Now I do. It's about founder's privilege. When Arabs claim the privilege to set Islam's agenda, they shed light on how intimidation has displaced intellect in Islam. As the Arab mind has become addled, so has the Muslim mind—as if all Muslims must walk (or hobble) in lockstep with the initial followers of the faith. "We're not smart enough" is a commonly uttered explanation throughout the Islamic world for why Muslims couldn't possibly have engineered the September 11 assaults. Zionist conspiracies also figure prominently in the whodunit chatter. It shouldn't astonish us that these theories are reflexively spouted in the Middle East, where Israel is the intimate enemy. But the conviction that the Jews orchestrated September 11 is more confidently creeping into Pakistan, Central Asia, and the immense, traditionally pluralist Muslim communities of Southeast Asia, where Arab grudge matches have no business coloring Islam. Unless, as I said, Muslims today are not so much an international community as an Arabian tribe.

In an Arabian tribe, lowly members must pledge uncritical allegiance to the sheikhs. One's sense of identity, if not security, depends on conformity. Maybe that's why the Palestinian–Israeli conflict, a regional war by all rational accounts, has become the litmus test of worldwide Muslim unity. A thoughtful assessment of the facts is not only irrelevant, but also inadvisable. Taking the right side, in deference to tribal bonds, matters most. Veteran journalist Fareed Zakaria corroborates my point in his 2003 book, *The Future of Freedom*. "Indonesian Muslims, who twenty years ago did not know where Palestine was, are today militant in their support of its cause. The Arab influence extends even into the realm of architecture. In its buildings the Islamic world has always mixed Arabic influences with local ones—Hindu, Javan, Russian. But local cultures are now being ignored in places such as Indonesia and Malaysia because they are seen as insufficiently Islamic (meaning Arab)."

Maybe it's the desert mind-set that manufactured dhimmitude, the systematic repression of Jews and Christians in Muslim lands. Why, even at the height of our tolerance, have Muslims treated certain peoples as inferior? What led to discriminatory documents like the Pact of Umar? It's got to be more than the Koran, which allows for love of non-Muslims. What, then, has tipped the scales toward bigotry? Let me propose this much: Equality can't exist in the desert, not if the tribe's integrity is to remain intact.

In that regard "we need a lot of self-criticism," Dr. Eyad Sarraj told me from the parlor of his ornate Gaza home in July 2003. He's the founder of the Gaza Community Mental Health Programme. He's also a Palestinian whose candor has driven Yasser Arafat to arrest him. Dr. Sarraj goes on about the self-inflicted fear and guilt that mangle Israelis into oppressors, and then he volunteers something about his own people: "I know we have a lot of psychopathology. It's a male-dominated society, there is no role for women, there is no freedom of expression, there is a heavy atmosphere of intimidation. . . . This is a tribal structure in which dissent is seen as treason. We have not yet developed a state of citizenry, within all the Arab countries, in which people are equal before the law. This is very serious."

I believe it. Raja Shehadeh couldn't speak his mind in Ramallah because, as he himself confesses, the elaborate web of social relationships in Palestinian culture squelches the individual. People find themselves more or less fixed in a chain with scant space for a weak link—a dissenting voice. You risk your life when you stand out because your destiny isn't yours at all; it's owned by the tribe. Your honor isn't yours alone; stepping out of line dishonors your kin and often your kind.

Maybe the grip of desert tribalism is why Palestinian suicide bombers rely on handouts from Arab despots. The paternalism of the desert tribe means that welfare trickles down at the discretion of the sheikhs. And maybe the desert personality of Islam is why a Muslim woman can be raped to compensate a dishonored clan, even if that clan's honor was violated not by her but by someone else. Because a woman belongs to her family, raping her is shaming her family, making the woman a fitting pawn in family blood feuds.

"That's not Islam!" some of you will protest. Practices throughout the Muslim world combine religious and nonreligious traditions!" Fair enough, which is why the question becomes: Can the norms of the desert be dislodged from Islam? If not, we have no hope in hell of reform.

As you think about that, I challenge you to answer this: Why would religion be so hard to extricate from local customs—tribal customs—if there wasn't something profoundly tribal about Islam to begin with? Every religion has its insular types, its tribes of the soul and mind. What must be stripped from Islam is its desert strain of tribalism, which takes the act of closing ranks to a crushing level.

Gaber Asfour is an Egyptian writer who winces at how the "Islam of the desert," as he calls it, is creeping into his own country's tradition of boisterous back-and-forth exchange. Desert Islam, he points out, opposes "the pluralistic, haggling life of the *el-haraa*—the urban alleyway bazaars. It is fanatic." Like seventh-century Bedouins, who anticipated a vendetta against them at every turn, desert-inspired Islamists immediately suspect, even hate, the "other." This means Jews. It means Westerners. It means women, whom Asfour says are regarded by the desert culture as a "source of temptation and evil." He claims that Saudi Arabia's oil money has helped spread the harsh habits of the desert. No doubt. But I think these habits have shaped Islam for a lot longer than we let on.

Taslima Nasrin, a feminist writer and doctor exiled from Bangladesh, gave me a concrete example of what she experienced well before the Saudis got rich. "As a child," she said, "I was told that Allah knows everything. Everything means *everything*. So Allah should know Bengali, shouldn't He?" She asked her mother, "How come I have to pray in Arabic? When I want to talk to Allah, why do I have to use somebody else's language?" Her mother didn't offer reasons, only routines. "She memorized from the Koran because it's written in the hadiths that when you die, two angels will come and ask questions of the soul. The answers will have to be given in Arabic; otherwise, your grave will squeeze you so hard. Why wouldn't those angels know Bengali? It's as if God occupied the minds of Muslims, invaded them." For her adult challenges to religious occupation, Nasrin was forced to flee her home in 1994. She now lives at an undisclosed location in Sweden.

Her mother's reverence for Arabic recalls that of Mr. Khaki and countless other Muslims. I've never understood this—the reverence, not just the language. Do Christians make each other feel inadequate for not knowing Greek, the original language of the New Testament? There was a time when the Christian worship service could only be performed in Latin, which protected the power of the Vatican's clerics. Muslims have no Vatican. But so what? I, like Taslima Nasrin, was told to communicate with God in a tongue that may as well have been Greek to me. Why should Arabic be irreplaceable? Sure, Allah's first word to the Prophet was "Read!" and Arabic is what he read. However, as I said earlier, Muhammad was illiterate. That's no secret among Muslims. His ability to read at God's command indicated the working of a miracle, not the supremacy of his native language.

Seems to me that in Islam, Arab cultural imperialists compete with God for the mantle of the Almighty. The Koran insists that "to God belongs the east and the west. Whichever way you turn there is the face of God." Why, then, *must* Muslims bow to Mecca five times a day? Isn't that a sign of being desert-whipped?

Call me superficial, but desert tribalism can be detected even in what Muslims are often instructed to wear. Millions of Muslim women outside of Arabia, including the West, veil themselves. They accept that it's an act of spiritual submission. It's closer to cultural capitulation. Do you know where Iranian women got the design for their post-revolutionary chadors—the ones that don't let you reveal a wisp of hair? From a mullah who led Shias in Lebanon. Now that's a heavy-duty import. While the Koran requires the Prophet's wives to veil, it never decrees such a practice for all women. Why, indeed, should it? Veils protect women from sand and heat—not exactly a pressing practical concern beyond Arabia, Saharan Africa, and the Australian outback. This means I could wear a turtleneck and base-ball cap to meet the theological requirements of dressing modestly. To cover my face because "that's what I'm supposed to do" is nothing short of a brand victory for desert Arabs, whose style has become the most trusted symbol of how to package yourself as a Muslim woman. Tell me: Should Allah operate like Prada?

To parrot the desert peoples in clothing, in language, or in prayer is not necessarily to follow the universal God. But you wouldn't know it by the myths with which Islam has been propagated through the centuries. These myths have turned non-Arab Muslims into clients of their Arab masters—patrons who must buy what's being sold to them in the name of Islamic "enlightenment."

To me, the most galling of these myths is *jahiliyah,* the moral darkness that's said to have existed before Islam's arrival. I recently cracked open a book at a relative's place in Toronto. It referred to the pre-Islamic period as the Age of Ignorance—capital A, capital I. Granted, the seventh-century Arabian peninsula baked in depravity and violence, sparking the need for a unifying faith. I don't disagree there. But the Koran speaks of moral backwardness only in the context of *Arab* history. The charade is, Arabs have assumed that the various non-Arab peoples they've conquered were also morally ignorant. The conquered have effectively been taught that because the Koran attributes darkness to the pre-Islamic period, all wisdom prior to Muhammad carries the weight of blasphemy and applies to every Muslim, outside of Arabia no less than inside. This myth is what made Taslima Nasrin's mother a religious robot, memorizing Arabic with the guilt of a sinner.

V. S. Naipaul, like Fareed Zakaria, has seen the consequences on a wider scale. Several years ago, Naipaul recounted his travels through Iran, Pakistan, Malaysia, and Indonesia. While acknowledging their struggles with European colonizers, he "was soon to discover that no colonization had been so thorough as the colonization that had come with the Arab faith. . . . It was an article of the Arab faith that everything before [it] was wrong, misguided, heretical; there was no room in the heart or mind of these believers for their pre-Mohammedan past." I've listened to more than a few Muslims write off Naipaul as a racist. That's ironic, because his point helps explain why, at my madressa, I never heard about the Jewish and Christian sources of many Islamic traditions. To recognize these influences would imply that the world didn't suffer from total foolishness before Islam, that Arab Muslims have borrowed from their predecessors, that they're hybrids with a debt to others rather than pure revolutionaries. But to say so is to defy the tribe. We can't have that, can we?

Well, maybe we can. Consider the taboo question of whether the Koran is authored by God from start to finish. During the first decades of Islam, with little time to have digested their new faith, Arabs scored international military successes in the name of Allah. It's conceivable that the compilation of the Koran had to be rushed to meet imperial pressures. In a groundbreaking investigative essay titled "What is the Koran?" *The Atlantic Monthly* told the story of an army general returning from Azerbaijan. The general warned Prophet Muhammad's third successor, Uthman, that converts were starting to bicker about what the Koran says. He pleaded with the caliph to "overtake this people" before they succumbed to dissension, just as the Jews and Christians had. Uthman ordered a fast turnaround on the Holy Book. Memorized revelations would be written down and scattered parchments of scripture would be assembled, all to be distributed as one version of the Koran. The "imperfect" or unofficial copies were to be destroyed. Question: Having been hastily approved, what if the "perfect" version was less than perfect?

It stands to reason that the Koran has imperfections. The rapidity of Arab empire-building would have crystallized priorities, making religion a servant of colonization and not the other way around. Might some verses of the Koran have been manipulated to meet political timetables and goals? Isn't it also plausible that

Arab warriors, more familiar with their sturdy customs than with their novel faith, grafted many of these customs onto the Islam they exported? It's not hard to see how the cultural baggage of desert Arabs, such as tribal walls, would pose as Islam proper. Nor is it difficult to imagine how an expedient Islam would become an obedient Islam—obedient less to God than to His gladiators.

But the clench of tribalism eased up in the early centuries of Islam and ingenuity flourished. How do we account for the golden age of trade, debate, and cultural cross-fertilization? What produced an open-hearted scientist and philosopher such as Al-Kindi, who offered "the utmost gratitude" to "former generations and foreign peoples" because "if they had not lived, it would have been impossible for us, despite all our zeal, during the whole of our lifetime, to assemble these principles of truth . . ."? In short, what went right? I wonder if it was the concept of a future.

Accumulating military victories meant that Arabs felt they had an appreciable and secured future. Which, in turn, meant that Islam didn't need to be thoroughly rigid or in-your-face. Better, in fact, that Islam be malleable so that the swiftly expanding empire could be massaged and managed. It's true that you couldn't separate religion from politics, but you could separate absolutism from prestige. The realization that absolutism doesn't bring prestige may be what fired up ambitious emirs to engage the best minds of the day—those of Jews and Christians, of course, but also those of non-Arab Muslims. It was non-Arabs who created the vast corpus of Islamic law up to and during the golden age. Some 135 schools of thought blossomed early on. The moral might be that Arab Muslims struck a balance between their tribal past and a pluralistic future.

When Arab Muslims lost their empire, they also forfeited the balance between past and future, tribalism and tolerance. They went down in battle after battle against non-Arabs—from the Berbers to the Mongols, from the Crusaders to the Ottoman Turks. These defeats inflicted humiliation on veteran Arab fighters. Beyond that, however, their brains took a beating. In the thirteenth century, the Mongols reportedly flung millions of manuscripts into the Tigris River, whose waters, as one maudlin Muslim puts it, "turned black for many days because of the ink and the blood." As for the Crusaders, they resorted to mammoth bonfires, with bishops torching as many as eighty thousand idea-laden volumes at one time. There's a metaphor here for how Arabs came to view their future: drowned, incinerated, or appropriated. They needed a healing balm.

The only undisputed glory that desert Arabs could now claim was the glory of Islam's founding moment. That the Koran emerged from the heartland of Arabia, in the language of Arabia, signified that Allah's "final" revelations would forever belong to the representatives of Arabia. Nobody else could get as close, geographically or spiritually. Therein lay dignity, even salvation, after such a spectacular free fall. But this balm was a bomb. The crucial equilibrium between past and future steadily degenerated into a defensive preoccupation with the past—and, in particular, into a fixation on the founding moment. I call it *foundamentalism.*

FOUNDAMENTALISM HAS FED SEVERAL TRAGEDIES. THE CLERGY, Islam's arrivistes, became Islam's de facto gatekeepers. With the gates of ijtihad—independent thought—closing by the twelfth century, muftis were already gaining the power to patrol the truth. As the truth narrowed, their mandate bloated, becoming nearer to that of soldiers than of scholars. All types of innovation became suspect and eventually banned. As guardians of the founding moment, clerics went back to the original "perfect" texts, the Koran and the hadiths, for proof that it's forbidden to seek any additional knowledge. Among the Prophet's sayings that they brought into vogue: "Beware of new things, for every new thing is an innovation and every innovation a mistake." Great way to build a future, don't you think?

The muzzle on innovation should have been limited to Arabia, if it had to be introduced at all. Instead, the anti-innovation rule hit Muslims well beyond the desert. In 1579, for example, Istanbul got an observatory. In 1580, clerics had it demolished. For all its fame, notes Muslim scholar Murad Hofmann, even Cairo's Al-Azhar University "was incompetent in the field of science." What a plunge from only a few centuries before, when Islam led the world in astronomy, math, medicine, and more. Perversely, this turn of events vindicates the man who started Istanbul's— and the Islamic universe's—first printing press in 1728. "It is vital for the Muslims, formerly in advance of the West in sciences, not to let themselves be eclipsed," said Ibrahim Muteferrika in his application for a business license. By 1745, he had to close shop. Mullahs prohibited the printing press.

It's not as if Muslim creativity ground to a standstill. In the early twentieth century, for example, a Persian princess briefly sparked a feminist consciousness (or a nationalist one, at any rate) that overhauled her state's constitution. She even attracted support from imams. Yeah, from men. In Isfahan, Iran, in Agra, India, in Fez, Morocco, in Sarajevo, Yugoslavia—each city cosmopolitan to the core—calls for stark religiosity had little traction. They also didn't make sense to specific sects within Islam. As Karen Armstrong stresses, "The Ismailis—a branch of the Shia—were urged to seek the truth wherever it could be found; Sufis had a great devotion to the Prophet Jesus, and the Faylasufs, who were inspired by the study of Plato and Aristotle, were seeking a more universal form of faith." But all these people and places existed on the periphery. Those distant from the desert didn't steer the general direction of Islam. Arabia did.

Here's one illustration. In the mid-nineteenth century, desert mullahs bullied the Ottoman Empire to drop three seminal issues of religious reform: ending the Muslim role in the African slave trade, freeing women from the yoke of the veil, and letting unbelievers live in the land of the Prophet. Mecca's chief cleric leveled a handy-dandy fatwa against these rumored changes emanating from Istanbul. "The ban on slaves is contrary to the Holy Sharia," he inveighed. "Furthermore . . . permitting women to walk unveiled, placing divorce in the hands of women, and such like are contrary to the pure Holy Law. . . . With such proposals the Turks have become infidels" and "it is lawful to make their children slaves." Although reformers, the Turks appeased Arabia's preachers. Istanbul's arch-mufti assured them that "certain impudent persons lustful for the goods of this world have fabricated strange lies and invented repulsive vanities" about what "the lofty Ottoman state was perpetrating—almighty God preserve us . . ." I emphasize "preserve" because petrifying Islam is pretty much the aim of the foundamentalists. As Muslims have slipped further behind Europeans in military and material honor, momentum has gathered for foundamentalism.

And that's the crowning tragedy of founding-moment mania. Religious "renewal" has become an exercise in constantly looking back. I do mean constantly—all the way back to the fourteenth century, when the Islamic empire began to fall into non-Arab hands. The first of the populist reformers, a Damascus intellectual known as Ahmed ibn Tammiya, denounced the Mongol invaders as apostates. That's because, even though they were converts to Islam, the Mongols supplanted the Sharia with their own laws. As ibn Tammiya saw it, no line between religion and government would have existed during Prophet Muhammad's time, which means the Mongols innovated. Unacceptable. Ibn Tammiya extended his lash to Muslim philosophy, mystical Sufism, and even Shia Islam. Each represented a post-Prophet innovation. "But ibn Tammiya died an outlaw," the historians among you might say. He also died an archetype, leaving a legacy to inspire—or incite—future "reformers." Which is what happened.

I'll give you a taste. In the 1950s and '60s, an Egyptian renegade named Sayyid Qutb took direct inspiration from ibn Tammiya. General Nasser hanged Qutb, but not before jailing him for several years. Qutb's jailhouse writings breathed fire into the modern Islamist movement, particularly the Muslim Brotherhood—the Koran-and-revolver gang I mentioned earlier. More recently, the Muslim Brotherhood ran the engineers union to which Mohamed Atta belonged.

And if that doesn't attest to ibn Tammiya's contemporary reach, get this: Sayyid Qutb's exiled brother, Muhammad, taught Osama bin Laden in Saudi Arabia. What did Osama learn? Among other things, that ibn Tammiya rose to prominence during a time of foreign invasion and went to his grave applauded by the Mongol-hating masses. Seven centuries after ibn Tammiya, we have bin Laden railing against the foreign invaders of the Prophet's homeland.

Today the invaders are Americans. Despite the Pentagon's 2003 announcement that most U.S. troops will be relocating from Saudi Arabia to Qatar, the disciples of ibn Tammiya would claim that crossing one border doesn't cleanse American soldiers of their colonialism—Qatar will always be part of the Prophet's peninsula. Riyadh must therefore be held to account for letting the Crusaders in at all. And that's another thing: Bin Laden has upped the emotional ante by depicting Americans as Crusaders, but he doesn't give two figs that the "Crusaders" have respected Saudi Arabia's ban on any public observance of Christianity. In 1990, when President George H.W. Bush visited U.S. troops stationed in Arabia, he agreed not to say Thanksgiving grace inside the country. Instead, the president led prayers aboard the U.S.S. *Nassau* in international waters.

That the Saudis have formed an alliance with the Great Satan only affirms to bin Laden the depth of defilement in the White House and the House of Saud. While America must be vanquished, so must its Saudi hosts. Bin Laden's mission is clear. In rescuing Muslims from both Houses, he's paying homage to the founding moment of Islam.

Is it mere happenstance that bin Laden spends so much time in caves, like the meditating Prophet Muhammad did? The Prophet could have indulged in the luxuries that his wife's wealth made possible, but he chose the simple life. Similarly, bin Laden cloaks himself in a riches-to-rags persona. Muhammad defected from one of Mecca's most prominent clans to profess his anti-establishment message. Bin Laden has estranged himself from his well-connected family. Muhammad challenged the moral basis of an entire economy by launching his mission in polyglot Mecca, a crossroads of commerce, where merchants could worship any god they wished. New York City is bin Laden's pre-Islamic Mecca. To him, people working in the World Trade Center were conscious combatants in the march of secular materialism, an ideology that worships gadgets and image-infested brands. That makes them guilty of idolatry and assault on the oneness of God. And that goes double for the capital-controlling Jews.

The parallels continue to proliferate. Muhammad's moral revolution took place at the same time as a technological one, in which state-of-the-art camel saddles permitted faster travel, more trade, greater greed, and deeper social disparities. Camel saddles yesterday, online transactions today. Muhammad raided the caravans of his enemies to nourish his army. Bin Laden's war chest has benefited from American consumers, who endlessly snort oil and opium.

Muhammad won decisive military victories through such primitive tactics as digging a ditch around his settlement, catching his opponents unawares, and crippling their combat-ready thoroughbreds. Bin Laden's cavalry used box-cutters to attack a superpower. Prophet Muhammad defined his nation as a politically engaged community whose borders would be delineated only by the reaches of faith. Bin Laden has cultivated a multinational network of operatives who transcend the maps drawn by foreign empires. Muhammad won the loyalty of Mecca's downtrodden before the elites realized his authority and converted. To be sure, bin Laden has a long way to go. In October 2001, half a million Pakistanis turned out to rally for moderation. However, we can't discount bin Laden's allure when, in the same month, a Gallup poll showed that 82 percent of urban Pakistanis considered him a freedom fighter.

Bin Laden's rationalizations might resonate with Muslims who revile their hedonistic and profligate leaders. His reenactment of the founding moment might even appeal to a mass Muslim hunger for redemption. But, in case it needs to be said, bin Laden's "reform" isn't reform. His Islam reinforces the vicious circle of repression in which Muslims have found themselves, with few exceptions, since the times of Arab conquest.

His is a tribal theology that equates unity with uniformity, vaulting a clutch of interpreters over individual, independent reasoning. Bin Laden offers nothing near an anti-imperial agenda. All he offers is more dictatorship from the desert.

THINK ABOUT WHERE BIN LADEN'S MISSION TOOK ROOT: SAUDI Arabia. He has turned only on its leaders, not on the country itself. This matters because Saudi Arabia's very existence springs from a pact between clerical and political interests. In the mid-1700s, a tribal chieftain named Muhammad ibn Saud approached a religious "reformer" named Muhammad ibn Abd al-Wahhab to strike a marriage of convenience. Bless my intent to forge a kingdom from pieces of the Arabian peninsula, he proposed to al-Wahhab, and I'll make you the new kingdom's spiritual guide. More accustomed to being run out of town by elites, al-Wahhab signed on. His "reformed" Islam, influenced by ibn Tammiya, has in turn influenced bin Laden. It's a spartan faith— scalped of its intellectual pedigree and relentlessly engaged in holy war. The jihadist justification allowed al-Wahhab's political partner, the tribe of ibn Saud, to raid territories and expand the kingdom over two hundred years. In 1932, from the debris of the Ottoman Empire, the formal Saudi state emerged. Its wholly undemocratic pact with Wahhabi mullahs remained firmly in place. So did its commitment to jihad. Through both of these things, Saudi Arabia has mastered the art of colonizing Muslims.

I want you to visualize the photos that come out of the hajj pilgrimage every year. Multiculturalism to the hilt, right? Now, add to this mural the fact that the Saudi king struts around as Custodian of the Two Holy Shrines. In his anointed capacity, he pretends to represent Muslims of every color, gender, and creed.

The real picture, however, isn't so pretty. How Riyadh treats Shias, Islam's second-largest denomination, can be summed up with one fact: According to official Saudi teachings, Shias are a Jewish conspiracy. Apparently, a Yemeni Jew schemed with other Jews to divide Islam and plant talmudic ideas in the minds of confused Muslims. The duped went on to become Shias.

As an offshoot of Judaism, Shias rank as dhimmis, don't they? Logically, then, that's the status they have in Saudi Arabia. Recently, a Shia Ismaili Muslim testified to the U.S. Congress about what happened when the Saudis annexed his hometown of Najran. "Not only were the Najranis religiously subjugated," said Ali Alyami, "but the means of their livelihood were reduced drastically. Most of their fertile farmland was expropriated by the Wahhabi governors, emirs, and judges. In addition, Wahhabis forcefully took half of what Ismailis produced from their farms and animals . . ." Notice the eerie echoes between this scene and what the Jewish peasants of Muhammad's time endured. It's all "permissible" if you believe that Shia Muslims are actually Jews.

Shias can't be represented in a Saudi court. Nor can anyone but a Wahhabi be appointed to the bench. Let's put two and two together: In Saudi Arabia, Shias stand before judges who are already convinced that they're heretics. So much for the 1990 Islamic human rights charter signed in Cairo by Muslim countries. It states that everyone is entitled to a fair trial. Everyone, I suppose, except non-Muslims. Since Shias are Jews . . . oy, the mind boggles.

Likewise, women in the kingdom can't show up in court even if they're accused of murder. They "have the legal status of a car," explains Ali Al-Ahmed, executive director of the U.S.-based Saudi Institute. And yet, they're not allowed to drive a car. Both realities reflect the fact that women, 57 percent of Saudi

Arabia's population, are considered minors in perpetuity. "They're transferred from their fathers' custody to their husbands' or sons'," Al-Ahmed points out. The *muttawa,* or religious police, trail these adult-minors constantly to enforce punctilious compliance with the law. That includes not wearing red on Valentine's Day—a crime inviting arrest.

In March 2002, compliance meant that young women couldn't escape a school fire until after they'd thrown on their full-length *abayas.* According to Saudi Arabia's own news reports, fifteen female students died and dozens sustained injuries when religious police forced the girls back into the burning building to retrieve their abayas, which literally became body sacks. A Saudi acquaintance of mine, doubting the truth of eyewitness accounts, said that domestic newspapers published this story simply to make trouble for the education minister. How does a state-controlled press just "make trouble"? The fact is that this horrific incident compelled Saudi journalists to challenge the status quo. They have every reason to do so: No other country in the world requires women by law to cover their faces. No other country in the world has the hubris to treat its female citizens as clones of Prophet Muhammad's wives—the only women obliged by the Koran to wear veils.

Looking for more ways in which Saudi Arabia's social contract reeks of stale tribalism? Power rests with a covey of senior princes. They're the ones who formulate policy and dispense favors to the mafia of mullahs whose loyalty they must maintain in order to avert an all-out rebellion. So, should we be astonished that the websites of Western news outlets are routinely blocked, but sites that profess hate, violence, and terrorism are easily accessed from the homeland of the Prophet? Is it any wonder that, until the media spotlight grew too glaring to ignore, Riyadh wouldn't audit Islamic charities operating from Saudi soil? Does it disturb us a scintilla that the Saudis wreck historical buildings, such as the mosques used by early Muslims, because these attractions might become false gods—like the World Trade Center's twin towers? And is it because clerics are to be far more protected than are the people that Saudi Arabia has never adopted the United Nations Declaration on Human Rights? In 1948, only the Eastern bloc and minority-ruled South Africa declined to sign on to the Declaration. Since then communism has collapsed. South Africa has reformed. Meanwhile, Saudi Arabia has gone global with its promulgation of an arid, absolutist Islam.

The results are in from Sudan and Pakistan, where too many madressas teach only the text of the Koran. You already know about Sudan's massacre and enslavement of non-Arab Muslims, as well as non-Muslims. When watching for Bedouin-style tribalism in Pakistan, you can't neglect this either: Some non-Muslims there face execution for having the nerve to utter the standard greeting of Islam—*as-salaam alaykum,* or "peace be with you." Yet another peace offer rebuffed.

Heading further east, desert Islam contorted Afghanistan in Saudi Arabia's theocratic image. Under the Taliban, the so-called Islamic Emirate of Afghanistan imitated the Saudi model of religious police, the Saudi approach to repressing women and Shias, and even the Saudi pattern of blowing up iconic religious sites to ward off idol worship. In Bangladesh, too, the statues of Christians, Hindus, and Buddhists are being singled out for destruction. Bangladesh is a democracy—on paper. Let's learn from the Bamiyan Valley Buddhas: Sitting in silence, praying for peace, won't be enough to fight desert Islam.

The Wahhabi world tour has already come to North America. Remember my battles to access the paltry library of my mosque in Richmond, British Columbia? Lo and behold, female students face the same strictures at a major Islamic school based in the United States and financed by the Saudis. As for being taught not to make friends with Jews, evidently I wasn't alone. Here's a passage straight out of an Arabic-language textbook distributed by the Saudis to Muslim schoolchildren in America: "The unbelievers, idolaters and others like them must be hated and despised. . . . We must stay away from them and create barriers between us and them."

Desert Islam is also encroaching on Southeast Asia. Islam came there through merchant trade, not military conquest. That may be why Southeast Asian Muslims have traditionally coexisted with Buddhists, Taoists, Christians, Sikhs, Hindus, Confucians—and women. But Middle Eastern money is transforming more than the landscapes of Malaysia and Indonesia. Laws and liberties are mutating too. In 1996, for example, police arrested three Muslim entrants in the Miss Malaysia Petite contest. The girls' families hadn't heard of the fatwa against Muslim participation in beauty pageants. When they found out, they couldn't believe their ears because such a prohibition didn't square with a country that has thrived on tolerance.

Since the mid-1990s, most of Malaysia's states have adopted Sharia laws that make it a crime to dispute any fatwa. If they don't nab you for temerity, they'll get you with timidity. "[V]ery few Muslims have the courage to question, challenge or even discuss Islam in public," writes Zainah Anwar, a member of the Malaysian feminist network Sisters in Islam. "They have been socialized to accept that the religious authorities know best." She, on the other hand, wants "to be a woman, a good Muslim and listen to the B-52s loud. I don't see any contradiction in that."

THE HIDDEN UNDERBELLY OF ISLAM · 155

It wasn't Zainah Anwar's version of Islam that drove the Miss World Beauty Pageant out of Nigeria in 2002. That fiasco, while easy to snicker about, spun off into several church-burnings and more than fifty deaths. I asked myself if this is how far desert Islam has spread. Did obsession with the founding moment fuel the antipageant riots? After all, Miss Nigeria had won the previous year's contest, giving her country the right to host the next one. Nigeria's Muslims knew this all along. Rioting started only after a journalist implied that Prophet Muhammad would have gotten a kick out of the pageant and taken its winner as his wife. An imprudent comment, to be sure, but one worthy of murder and banditry? When people are indoctrinated to believe that any aspect of the founding moment is sacred, then the faith is destined to become static, brittle, inhumane. In this case, so inhumane that even though the offending newspaper apologized three times, Muslim protestors set its offices aflame. One more thing: The columnist who got cheeky about Prophet Muhammad had, a few weeks before, scolded Christians and invoked the name of Christ along the way. Nobody died.

Foundamentalism is killing us—and a whole lot of others as well. Folks, who cares how closely we approximate the founding moment? To be consumed by this—no, even to wink at this—is terminal. The time has come to take a hint from Kemal Ataturk, the architect of modern Turkey. In 1925 he proclaimed, "I flatly refuse to believe that today, in the luminous presence of science, knowledge, and civilization in all aspects, there exist . . . men so primitive as to seek their material and moral well-being from the guidance of one or another sheikh." Ataturk proved himself a visionary precisely by jettisoning any association with Islam's founding moment. He didn't play the purity game because it can produce only one winner: the bearded guy who reduces everything to what's already been said, seen, and tried. For any society to grow, Ataturk knew, it has to hold out the possibility of many winners in many fields.

His snub of the founding moment has produced a democracy in Turkey. Despite being vulnerable to the whims of the military, and flawed in a host of other ways, it's still the Muslim world's most mature democracy. And devout Muslims who take part in its political life can be winners, too—in November 2002, Turks elected an Islamist party as their government. Now for a second telling point: The popularity of Turkey's Islamists didn't depend on opposing U.S. foreign policy or castigating Israel. It had to do with promising to create jobs and stem corruption. Voters in Bahrain voiced those exact priorities when they went to the polls a month earlier—the first election in the Arab gulf in which women could vote. These voters identified a future and not just a past.

Given the chance to speak, many Muslims will say they don't want to keep replicating the founding moment. They want less of the road already taken and more of the road forward. When enraged Pakistani parents chase away clerics who recruit their sons into criminal activity, you see their desperation to embark on the road forward. When moderate Indonesian Muslims put out a book called *The New Face of Husband-Wife Relations,* attempting to reconcile Islam with human rights, you know the road forward has a few more travelers. When hard-liners storm out of Iran's parliament to protest the influence of student rallies for reform, you know the future is gathering steam. When the *Arab News,* a Saudi English-language daily, publishes a column detailing how much more economically advanced Israelis are than Arabs, and when that column screams, "Face the Facts, Arabs," you know the gag is loosening. Tribal silences, like delusions, are ready to dissolve, even at official levels. As Jordan's foreign minister wrote recently in the *New York Times,* "Arab leaders must finally take a public stand against suicide bombings" while making "political and economic systems more democratic."

When a Lebanese journalist writes that "the ball is in Washington's court" to support the "green shoots of democracy" germinating in the Middle East, you know that he's inviting a global declaration of interdependence. When Arab intellectuals join with the U.S. State Department to condemn a blatantly anti-Semitic Egyptian TV series, you know that interdependence has a fighting chance. The greater the diplomatic pressure from the West, the more emboldened are the internal voices for change.

And when the king of Morocco announces an overhaul of Sharia law that eliminates polygamy while giving women access to divorce, alimony, and custody—reforms based on the Koran itself—then you know faith can outwit custom. Above all, when North America incubates a group such as the Progressive Muslim Union, whose platform affirms "the equal status and worth of all human beings," calls for "critical inquiry and dynamic engagement" with Islam's guiding texts, and declares that "there are multiple paths that lead to truth," then you know the freedoms of the West can impel a new generation of Muslims to revive ijtihad, Islam's lost tradition of creative thinking.

The road forward, it seems to me, must try to tackle three challenges at the same time: first, to revitalize Muslim economies by engaging the talents of women; second, to give the desert a run for its money by unleashing varied interpretations of Islam; and third, to work with the West, not against it. In each instance, what we're undermining is hoary tribalism.

I hereby cease to be a refusenik. Sign me up for Operation Ijtihad.

7

OPERATION IJTIHAD

It might appear ridiculous that someone who's not a theologian, a politician, or a diplomat (in any sense of the word) has the chutzpah to comment on what could be done to reform Islam. On occasion, I've felt presumptuous just thinking about it—but only on occasion. I don't care to "know my place." Change has to come from somewhere. Why not from a young Muslim woman who's got no investment, emotional or otherwise, in defending the status quo?

Here's what I'd picked up so far. Muslims constantly exhibit a knack for degrading women and religious minorities. Could both of these troubles be tackled at the same time? I'd teased out enough strands of hope from the Koran, as well as from history, to believe in the possibility of reform. For instance, Muslims have a centuries-old love affair with commerce, which piqued my interest for two reasons. First, trade has always helped grease the wheels of good relations among Muslims, Jews, and Christians. Second, there's no prohibition in the Koran against women becoming businesspeople. My tentative conclusion: God-conscious, female-fueled capitalism might be the way to start Islam's liberal reformation. But did anyone else think such an idea could work?

One afternoon, in October 2002, I caught an episode of *The Oprah Winfrey Show* about the sorry state of the Muslim sisterhood worldwide. Oprah gave airtime to a woman who faced death by stoning, another disfigured by a splash of acid, and a third who said that in her society, she had the worth of a shoe—no more and no less. "What can we do?" Oprah bluntly asked the camera.

The director cut to Zainab Salbi, one of Oprah's guests. "I had an Afghan woman who said that with $100 she can start an income-generating business. . . ." Salbi, head of a global advocacy group for women, appealed to the TV audience as she continued to speak about the Afghan entrepreneur. "Help her learn to read and write so she does not sign papers" to abdicate custody of her children. "Help her know her rights, so she can tell her husband or the [tribal] chief: 'No, you cannot do that to me.' Help her lead her own fight!" Salbi proposed that women in the West invest in the business acumen of women in the Muslim world. When women have money that they've earned themselves, she suggested, they're more likely to begin the crucial task of questioning their lot.

For me, this talk-show moment shouted self-help, but it was also about dignity—and, ultimately, about religious reform. As Muslim women start to question, they shift from being badges of family "honor" to being dignified humans. "Honor" demands sacrificing your individuality to maintain the reputation, status, and prospects of your husband, father, and brothers. But to question this existence is to assert that you're not communal property.

You're your own person, acting in your own name, expressing your own thoughts and communicating them in your own voice. You have dignity. And the beauty is, that's what Prophet Muhammad wanted all along for Muslims—that we transcend tribe, with its inward-looking, contagiously neurotic impulses; the very impulses that made seventh-century Arabia a wasteland of inequity, enmity, and violence. By liberating Muslim women's entrepreneurial talents, we in the twenty-first century can help transform honor into dignity and thereby reform how Islam is practiced.

Supporting female entrepreneurs would be goal number one of Operation Ijtihad, a campaign to jump-start change in Islam.

I'm not nominating myself as the leader of this yet-to-be-born campaign. Actually, I don't think there should be one leader. Unshackling the Muslim world is an ambitious effort that will require an array of allies, Westerners among them, if only to deal a decisive blow to tribalism. The stakes demand a cross-cultural vision. September 11 is a searing reminder of what can happen when we hive ourselves off from the problems of "others," the lesson being that good global citizenship has colossal benefits for domestic security. Regardless of whether Westerners want to accept this fact, Westerners have to accept it.

And we have to accept it *now* because Arab Muslims are experiencing a baby boom. About 60 percent of the people in Arab states are under twenty years old, compared to just 29 percent in America. Plenty of young Arab Muslims have college degrees, but most have no prospects for work. You know that can't be good news. The idle often gravitate to radical organizations that promise free food, purposeful activity, and a release valve for anger. Give it one more generation and Arab Muslim numbers are projected to increase by 40 percent—from almost

300 million today to 430 million in 2020. Whoever denies these kids economic and civic participation will incite a degree of chaos capable of convulsing much of the planet. The Arab baby boom is as much the West's problem as it is the Middle East's.

Half of all Arab youth surveyed by the United Nations in 2001 said they want to move, and they're eagerly looking West. Eagerly enough that in 2000, Australia ran a dissuasion campaign in the Middle East and Central Asia to warn illegal immigrants about the crocodiles, snakes, and insects they could encounter upon arriving. But, by the same token, the West can't advance without immigrants. The populations of the European Union, America, Japan, Canada, and Australia are rapidly aging and only faintly fertile. These regions need new workers to keep consumerism up, taxes rolling in, and social services paid—especially for the elderly. In short, the West needs Muslims.

What the West doesn't need are more Mohamed Attas. The Hamburg student and September 11 hijacker swallowed his spoon-fed Koran as he would a course in computer programming. Despite his mildly secular upbringing, his Egyptian degree in engineering, and his German postgraduate schooling, Atta seemed incapable of (or uninterested in) questioning Islam's autocratic interpreters. Yet the West needs Muslims who ask the tough questions, and waging Operation Ijtihad abroad will be central to this aim. Why wait until millions more Muslims show up at Australian, German, and North American checkpoints? Isn't it a basic matter of security that Muslims heading to these places arrive already knowing that Islam can be observed in ways that complement pluralism rather than suffocate it? How, then, do we sow reform in the Muslim world— without becoming cultural colonizers?

· · ·

OPERATION IJTIHAD BEGINS WITH EMPOWERING MORE MUSLIM women to become businesspeople. Since the 1980s, Muhammad Yunus has been confirming that the Islamic world can, indeed, produce female entrepreneurs by giving them access to minimal start-up funds. A Bangladeshi economist, Yunus founded the Grameen Bank. *Grameen* is the Bengali word for "village," and this bank loans tiny amounts of money to people whom the standard lenders consider untouchable—especially the landless, who are mostly women. According to the *No-Nonsense Guide to International Development,* "Thirty-one million people, three-quarters of them women and two-thirds classified as the 'poorest of the poor,' have received micro-loans in more than forty countries" since the Grameen Bank opened. It has financed businesses that manufacture everything from cosmetics and candles to bread, umbrellas, mosquito nets, even mobile phones. And the loan repayment rate? Ninety-eight percent, thanks in large part to the peer pressure that exists in villages to keep the community's reputation clean. That's a healthier way to channel tribal impulses than what most Muslim women are used to. Contrast that repayment rate to the 10 percent recovery boasted by the Bangladesh Industrial Development Bank, which serves only people with property. No contest.

So here's a concept for launching Operation Ijtihad: Imagine if the United States, the European Union, Canada, Australia, Japan, and other rich allies took a sliver of their national security budgets and pooled them into a program of micro-enterprise loans for women throughout the Muslim world.

This doesn't qualify as imperialism. The loans wouldn't be foisted on anyone, they'd be available to those women who see an unmet need in their communities and believe they can fill that need through ingenuity. As an example, take the villager who inspired Yunus to invent the Grameen Bank. A weaver of bamboo stools, she told Yunus that in order to purchase her raw materials, she had to borrow from the merchant who bought her finished product. Because she depended on his loans, he could fix the price of her stools, leaving her with a take-home pay of two cents a day. What's imperialistic about giving women the resources to end their serfdom? Remember, too, that Islamic tradition bustles with the sounds of business. As an old saying goes, "May your hajj be accepted, your sins be forgiven, and your merchandise not remain unsold." Commerce and religion are so intertwined that there's even a Koranic theory about when lenders can come collecting—namely, only when those in whom they've invested have created new wealth, but not a moment before.

Fortunately, micro-loans have a history of paying off, and America, at least, knows it. Every year for several years during Bill Clinton's presidency, the U.S. made 2 million such loans to struggling countries. As Clinton wrote in a 2002 issue of *New Perspectives Quarterly,* "That two million should rise to fifty million" all over the world. He stands by the value of micro-loans because he's witnessed their effect among rural Arkansas beauticians as well as African cattle-breeders. In the mid–1980s, Clinton recruited Yunus to create the Grameen-like Good Faith Fund for the people of Pine Bluffs, Arkansas. A few years later, and based on hundreds more success stories, a book was published called *Give Us Credit: How Muhammad Yunus' Micro-Lending Revolution Is Empowering Women from Bangladesh to Chicago.*

Ah, but do Muslim countries want any of this, or does Clinton assume too much? Looks like he's spoken with Hernando de Soto, a Nobel-nominated economist who's caught the attention of Indonesia, Pakistan, Algeria, and Egypt. Their governments are intrigued by de Soto's specialty—reviving "dead capital" in moribund economies. Two examples of dead capital are black market businesses, which operate off the books and off the tax rolls, and properties claimed by squatters, who have no clear title to the parcels of land on which they live. In each case, we're talking about assets that poor people can't afford to register legally because it takes too much government paperwork, time, and fees. Lose the red tape, de Soto has shown, and the capital of the enterprising lower classes can explode into something truly constructive. Squatters can get collateral to secure mortgages and build less provisional lives. Cash-only businesses can expand into legal and value-added companies. Governments can thereby acquire taxable income. Everybody wins, particularly women and children. They're usually the ones who stay home in order to guard untitled land. Men, after all, must work. When property is documented, though, women can leave the premises to sell goods at the market, for instance, and children can go to school. After Peru implemented de Soto's ideas, school attendance rose by 26 percent. No wonder a handful of governments in Muslim countries are now inviting de Soto to lend them an insight or two, and a thousand men turned up to hear him speak in Dubai. But his message resonates well beyond the establishment.

In the summer of 2002, the United Nations released its first *Arab Human Development Report*. Researched and written by Arabs themselves, it took Middle Eastern governments to task for neglecting the energies of half their populations: women. In fact, "women's empowerment" was one of three "deficits" that the report unearthed, the others being "knowledge" and "freedom." Reversing the first deficit can increase knowledge and freedom. Helping women achieve financial independence en masse will buttress their existing, often underground, attempts to become literate. They won't need to believe the oracles of the big boys if they can reach their own conclusions about what the Koran contains. How do I know women have an interest in interpreting for themselves? Old Afghan women, some of them refugees, now attend schools that younger women run, and that they ran in secret during the Taliban's time. "I want to find out if what the mullah says is in the Koran is really true," one elder told an American visitor about why she's learning to read.

Suppose, as an entrepreneur, this woman had assets to preserve. Then she'd have even more reason to learn to read. In an explicit passage that imams rarely publicize to the middle and lower classes, the Koran permits women to negotiate marriage contracts that meet their personal conditions. "If a woman fear[s] ill-treatment . . . on the part of her husband," says a verse in chapter 4, "it shall be no offense for them to seek a mutual agreement, for agreement is best. People are prone to avarice." Today, a woman's personal conditions for marriage might include: "My husband can't lay an unwanted finger on me or on my earnings. If he does, I'll regard it as 'ill-treatment' and I'll have the right to divorce him." What an incentive to turn that micro-enterprise loan into a serious success. He who tries to snatch it away will have an informed Koranic argument to answer, and a prenuptial agreement that Sharia judges can't easily bypass.

Men would benefit directly from Operation Ijtihad, since widespread entrepreneurship will encourage foreign investment. The infusion of outside money into local ventures is sure to reduce dependence on the military, security forces, and government bureaucracy—the three career ghettos in which so many Muslim men currently congregate. Richard Haass, the U.S. State Department's policy director, recognizes how men's dignity is bound up with women's. In December 2002, Haass told a Washington crowd that "[p]atriarchal societies in which women play a subservient role to men are also societies in which men play subservient roles to men." Gloria Steinem couldn't have said it better. Investing in women merchants may be everybody's best chance for busting the institutional monopolies that enrich clerics and their paymasters at the expense of ordinary people.

As an approach to liberalizing Islam, Operation Ijtihad seems promising. But the promise could sputter and ultimately stall as long as Islamic "human rights" codes enshrine men as the providers of their families, prohibiting women from earning money. And yet, I have to believe that prosperity, or the prospect of it, can shake up the consensus that men must be the ones to bring home the pork-less bacon. Allow me to illustrate how the need to make a living can motivate new thinking.

I'll start on a morose note. In 1997, Islamists wiped out fifty-eight tourists in Luxor, Upper Egypt. This massacre took place after years of lower-magnitude murder sprees—targeting some British tourists here, several Germans there, one or two Taiwanese. Luxor broke the camel's back because Egypt's tourism sector hemorrhaged up to $2 billion as a result of the killings. That's when Egyptian public opinion turned against the terrorists and in support of the sixteen-year-old Emergency Law, introduced to keep religious militants under pitiless surveillance. It's a bloody shame that the Emergency Law has rusted into a cudgel for political power-mongers, but that's not my point here. It's this: The moment terrorism threatened the economy, Egyptians threatened the terrorists.

When the opportunity for a better quality of life for everyone is offered through female entrepreneurship, the priorities of people could change—from tribalism to trade, from the honor of husbands as sole providers to the dignity of reciprocity between men and women. Maybe I'm overly optimistic, but the tourist trade could account for why we see hints of reciprocity between Israelis and Egyptians in the Sinai Peninsula. Israelis vacation in the Sinai. Egyptians appreciate the business. Muslims and Jews have relatively smooth relations there, testifying that, to a degree, commerce can forge more fluid social contracts.

Still, I don't underestimate the manipulative prowess of those who worship desert Islam. The means that foundamentalists marshal to stir hearts are outlined on the website of Women Living under Muslim Laws, a network of human rights activists. Foundamentalists, says the site, "have made enormously effective use of communication technologies. . . . Simple inexpensive audiocassettes of preachings that include tirades against women and against the supposedly Western values of equality and autonomy, and that incite people to violence and in extreme cases even to murder opponents, have flooded the streets and marketplaces of many Muslim communities. They are broadcast on public buses; on loudspeakers of mosques; and on the radio."

On highly accessible TV, too, such as Lebanon's Al-Manar channel, affiliated with Hezbollah and licensed by the Lebanese government since 1997. Al-Manar's mandate—"to enhance the civilized role of the Arab and Islamic community"—actually endorses Jew-bashing as a tactic of choice. The station's website features a program called *Inqilab al-Soura,* roughly translated as the "Conversion of Image." It's about media literacy, or so it seems until you wade through the show's description: "*Inqilab al-Soura* monitors all the Zionist Hebrew-speaking audiovisual media and press, thus exposing the status and hidden facts of the Zionist military warfare." For good measure, the program is produced and hosted by a "former detainee in Israeli prisons." Hey, at least there's life after Zionist torture. The last time I looked, the website promised to add a shopping section. Clearly, commerce can't be all there is to fighting the fundamentalists.

Media will have to be another front line of Operation Ijtihad. But instead of telling "America's story" better, which has proven to be an inflammable cocktail of vanity and irrelevance, what if the West financed media outlets that broadcast to Muslim audiences the stories of their own women entrepreneurs? David Hoffman is president of the Internews Network, a non-profit organization that aids independent media around the world. He applauds America's backing of local media in the former Soviet Union. "All told, more than 1,600 broadcasters and 30,000 journalists and media professionals have benefited from U.S.-sponsored training and technical assistance programs," Hoffman observed in the March 2002 issue of *Foreign Affairs* magazine. "More than a dozen national television networks emerged from these efforts, reaching more than 200 million viewers. As a result, citizens in every city of the former Soviet Union now have a variety of channels from which to choose."

What if a Western coalition of Muslims and non-Muslims endowed women in the Islamic world to own and manage local TV stations? What if Oprah Winfrey led the coalition? Oprah knows how it feels to be an outsider, doesn't let victimology paralyze her, and, above all else, is passionate about the education of women and children. Oprah's very presence would issue a stark screw-you to men who want to run everything of worth in Islamic countries. As a smart man told Oprah during the show about Muslim women, "Whether you like it or not, you're a catalyst." She didn't disagree. In any event, satellite dishes are proliferating in the world of Islam. What the printing press did for the Protestant reformation—relax the stranglehold on knowledge—indie TV channels can do for Islam.

We could begin modestly, with the tried-and-true means of radio broadcasts. For one thing, radio would protect identities in the critical early years of Operation Ijtihad. Not everybody wants to be picked out (and picked off) in the street as the one who said that Prophet Muhammad declared women to be partners with men rather than their subordinates. Some Muslims wouldn't want to be recognized as having shared the stories about Khadija, the Prophet's cherished first wife—fifteen years his senior and a wealthy, self-made merchant *who proposed to him*. It's said that even after submitting to God, largely on Khadija's counsel, Muhammad kept taking advice from her. These stories might be nonsense, more the products of legend or conjecture than of history. But I'm sure I'm not the only Muslim who hungers to hear freethinkers candidly debate their truth and pertinence on the airwaves. Dr. Ayesha Imam, a human rights advocate in Nigeria, says it's crucial to popularize discussions like these "so that people who have been profoundly uncomfortable about the very conservative nature of the new Sharia acts have a basis on which they can legitimately criticize, rather than feeling that they don't know enough to be able to speak." In other words, exploring doubts can feed confidence, including that of female entrepreneurs. Expressing doubt affirms the possibility that you can counter the tribe. If any "reform" initiative avoids introducing doubt, it will certify Islam as a religion not just for the hardhearted but also for the fainthearted—those with neither the guts to question nor the outlets to do so.

WHY APPEAL TO ISLAM AT ALL? IT'S A QUESTION POSED BY TASLIMA Nasrin, who adamantly believes that reform will emerge only when religion retreats. As far as she's concerned, Muslims need to replace religious laws with civil ones, completely separating mosque and state. But must Islamic countries imitate Judeo-Christian ones in order to be humane? I don't know. Those who say *yes* have a second challenge to address: The reality is that Islam forms a pillar of identity for millions of women. At the moment, taking religion out of the public sphere might be more than unrealistic; it might be unproductive as well.

Riffat Hassan, a professor of religious studies at the University of Louisville, has direct experience here. She explains, "If you ask an Afghan woman, 'Do you believe in universal human rights?' she will look at you blankly. If you ask her, 'Do you believe in God?' she will say, 'Yes.' If you ask her, 'Do you believe in a God who is just, merciful, and compassionate?' she will say, 'Yes.' If you ask her, 'Do you believe this God would want you to be beaten, to be brutalized?' she would instantly understand this and say, 'No.'" So, let's get practical. Do we want Muslim women to stand up for at least some of their human rights or, by virtue of being under nonreligious laws, do we want them to feel alienated? Antagonized? Betrayed?

Nor do educated women necessarily subscribe to Nasrin's dogmatic secularism. I recently met a young Muslim woman at a constitutional conference in Ottawa. A lawyer at the Department of Justice, she'd immigrated to the West in order to practice her faith more meaningfully. For her, that means choosing to wear the hijab—a choice blessed in North America but not in her native Tunisia, which has outlawed headscarves in public as part of an effort to "modernize."

My encounter with this lawyer prompted me to think about the balance involved in democratizing the Muslim world. It's almost counterintuitive to the secular mind, so follow closely. Voting with her head and not just her feet, the lawyer proved that even among young, learned Muslims, freedom to express faith openly remains a key expectation of democracy. Suppressing Islam for the sake of "progress" resembles tyranny. When the likes of Tunisia and Turkey impose walls between spiritual life and the material realm, they end up giving secular democracy a less-than-democratic name. Fundamentalists can then protest that the real political agenda isn't openness, but Westernization. And there's the rub: Fundamentalists expertly exploit the frustrations of people whose lives have been shocked by secularizing regimes. Holding elections in such climates often triggers more representation for the forces of desert Islam. Bye-bye democracy.

Before democracy can have legs in Arab Muslim countries, these countries need to be exposed to a competition of ideas. As I've been arguing, alternate interpretations of Islam can hold their own against the desert, even on the all-important symbolic level. That's if we can get alternate interpretations disseminated, debated, aired, re-aired—popularized.

I appreciate why Taslima Nasrin insists that secularization is the solitary hope. She doesn't think you can reaffirm the value of Islam without reinforcing its noxious air of supremacy. I hear her. That's why I've consulted anthropologists, sociologists, psychologists, theologians, and—what the hell—atheists about how human beings can curb our tendency to pursue victory instead of coexistence. Early in 2002, I attempted an experiment. In a mock memo to Yasser Arafat, published by a national newspaper, I floated an approach to sharing land that would let Muslim Palestinians retain dignity, identity, and integrity. I pointed out that the *hijra,* Prophet Muhammad's famous move from Mecca to Medina, translates into "seeking protection by settling in a place other than one's own." Jewish tribes had long lived in Medina, yet most of them shared their environs with the Prophet and his people. Yasser, I beseeched, take a leaf from history. Wouldn't it be tit for tat to share Palestine with the Jews, who, like the early Muslims, migrated in search of protection from murderous prejudice? I figured I had the beginnings of a breakthrough.

The next day, a letter appeared in the paper from a prominent Toronto Muslim. He wrote, "Hijra means seeking protection by settling in a place other than one's own, on the invitation of the inhabitants of the new place, i.e. not by force. Ms. Manji omitted the last qualifier to advance her argument." He was pointing out that some of Medina's tribes had invited the Prophet to arbitrate their disputes, making Medina a convenient place for him to go when fleeing the oppression of Mecca. His more subtle point was that Arabs didn't invite Jews to live among them in Palestine, so the hijra analogy can't apply.

The day after that, a Jew responded to the Muslim. She commended my reasoning, then turned her sights to Palestine. "[F]or those Muslims who proclaim that they were in the area before the Jews, I must remind them that Abraham and Sarah were living in Hebron when Sarah died long before the Prophet Muhammad existed." In one way or the other, we all have to be right, don't we? I lump myself into that group.

But if you're right, must I be wrong?

I asked that question of David Hartman, one of Israel's most authoritative rabbis. He replied with another question. "Is my vibrancy, is my life, a threat to yours?" Before I could respond, Rabbi Hartman answered for himself. "I mean, I love to hear Muslims pray. It wakes me up at four o'clock in the morning but, for the sake of pluralism, I'll kill my sleep. On Sunday, the church bells are ringing. I say, 'Fine. Bang away, kid.'"

And that's when it hit me—religion is one reason that Israel perseveres as a multifaith democracy in the midst of its own demagogues and a welter of Arab dynasties. Judaism, unlike Islam and Christianity, doesn't set out to convert. It harbors no claim to universalism. By its own laws, it can't evangelize. "That's because Jews are 'the chosen ones,'" Muslims are apt to sniff. "Chosen people don't need to prove themselves. Come hell or high water, their salvation is in the bag." I consider this a tragic misapprehension. Jews believe they're chosen, but not simply for raisins in heaven. They're also chosen for burdens on earth, and on behalf of all humanity. Whether Jews prove themselves capable of handling those burdens responsibly will determine if they deserve deliverance. Far from being "in the bag," salvation rests in being responsible. But what does that mean? I can only convey the mainstream Jewish consensus: Being responsible means resisting tribal arrogance.

As humans, Jews sometimes turn arrogance into a high art— or at least a gauche one. I recoil at the West Bank crazies who illuminate their hilltop settlements with brash, neon Stars of David. I'm heartsick at the Sharon government's consistent refusal to arrest the criminals who erect illegal settlements. I don't pretend to defend those Jews who kindle fires with branches severed from olive trees that Arab farmers have nurtured for decades, and who sequester themselves in yeshivas where they're forbidden to study the disciplines, from astronomy to philosophy, that made Maimonides tick. Bear in mind, though, that these folks are lightweights in contemporary Judaism. Infuriating, and growing in number, but still relatively marginal.

Jews who are mainstream, even prominent, sometimes exceed the call of responsibility—without acknowledgment from us Muslims. At a pro-Israel rally in April 2002, Paul Wolfowitz, the U.S. deputy defense secretary, handed a metaphorical olive branch to Palestinians. A noted hawk, Wolfowitz conceded that "innocent Palestinians are suffering and dying in great numbers as well." The gathering jeered. But what did Edgar M. Bronfman, president of the World Jewish Congress, do? He wrote to the *New York Times* with avowed humility. "Those who booed should be ashamed of themselves and should be made aware of the passage in the Haggadah [Passover story] . . . God chastises the angels for cheering as the Egyptians were drowning while chasing the Israelites who had crossed the Red Sea. God told them, These are my people, too. Palestinians are dying in this war in the Middle East. My sympathies are certainly for Israel and its people, but we must all be aware that Palestinians are people, too."

The same covenant to recognize the "other" allows Britain's chief Orthodox rabbi, Jonathan Sacks, to write about the "dignity of difference." Did I say write about it? More like write the book on it. In Sacks's prose, "God creates difference; therefore it is in one-who-is-different that we meet God." To Rabbi Sacks, "[t]he supreme religious challenge is to see God's image in one who is not in our image." I'll admit that Sacks has taken heat from ultra-Orthodox rabbis, particularly for his point that Judaism doesn't have the last word on Truth. Under pressure, Sacks has revised some sentiments. Not all, however. Not the ones about the sanctity of difference. For years, in fact, Rabbi Sacks has been promoting Jewish responsibility to the "other," all the while holding on to his seat as head of Britain's Orthodox Jews.

Why am I banging away at the humanity that Judaism enables? Because while I expect that Operation Ijtihad will spur conversations among the three Peoples of the Book, these "trialogues" will amount to something only if they're driven by talmudic open-endedness. I don't mean the Talmud itself; I mean the attitude, so elegantly voiced by Rabbi Hartman, that Abraham's God is equally the "God of surprise and novelty." A God, that is, whose will you can't predict.

Too preposterous a thought for most Arab Muslims? Malaysia's prime minister suggests that it is. At a 2002 international assembly of Muslims in Kuala Lumpur, Mahathir Mohamad let it slip that Islam's leadership can no longer come from Arabs because, on balance, they don't know how to speak with non-Muslims. But, he implied, Asian Muslims do. Ironically, Mahathir has betrayed his own susceptibility to Arab influences by holding Jews responsible for Malaysia's currency crisis and by standing on the sidelines as Sharia law spreads in his country. The good news is: Malaysia isn't Mahathir. Neither is neighboring Indonesia, the world's most populous Muslim country, where millions have condemned the Islamist bombing of a Bali nightclub. In fact, Southeast Asians have always had to practice Islam in an entrepot that's multiethnic (Chinese, Indian, Malay) and multifaith (Buddhist, Christian, Hindu, Muslim).

Likewise with Central Asians. In Kazakhstan, a Muslim-majority country carved out of the former Soviet Union, nearly one hundred ethnic groups commingle. There, secularism survives and tolerant Sufism thrives. There, Jews recently gathered for a conference hosted by the government—a conference that concluded with a joint Jewish-Muslim call for peace. There, the official English-language newspaper congratulated couples on

Valentine's Day. We're not in the Saudi sand dunes anymore. If Islam's heart is stronger than desert Arabia's value system, and sustainably so, Asian Muslims have an opportunity to demonstrate it by continuing their conversation with the "God of surprise and novelty."

I've got a second caveat about interfaith conversation. Whoever does the participating, such exchanges can be fraught with fraud. Consider the case of Muhammad Sayyid Tantawi, the sheikh of Al-Azhar Mosque. You can't get more prestigious than Al-Azhar. Fareed Zakaria describes it as "the most important center of mainstream Islam in the Arab world." Besides being mainstream Islam's top religious official, Sheikh Tantawi is patron of the UK-based Three Faiths Forum, an organiza-tion intended to help Christians, Jews, and Muslims achieve mutual understanding. Sounds pleasant, but let's sandblast the rhetoric and drill for what's underneath. In an April 2002 sermon translated by the Middle East Media Research Institute, Sheikh Tantawi characterized Jews as "the enemies of Allah, sons of pigs and apes." At a 1999 conference on nuclear strategy in Egypt, the sheikh exhorted Muslims to "acquire nuclear weapons as an answer to the Israeli threat" and promised that "[i]f Israel has nuclear weapons it will be the first to be defeated because it lives in a world in which there is no fear of death."

These statements shouldn't be brushed off as the toothless barks of a man aggravated to madness by the Palestinian morass. Even when the peace process was clinging to life, he made similar comments. In January 1998, the sheikh gave an interview to Al-Jazeera. He'd recently met with Israel's chief rabbi, a Cairo rendezvous that caused a flap in the Egyptian press. "Is there any benefit to these kinds of meetings?" wondered the Al-Jazeera presenter.

"Of course," crowed Sheikh Tantawi. "On the personal level, I attacked him and proved to him that Islam is the religion of truth. . . . I think that whoever refuses to meet with the enemy in order to slap him on the face is a coward, as long as the meeting in question serves Islam."

Is that also how our slap-happy sheikh views his patronage of the Three Faiths Forum? As an opportunity to thwack more Jews? Or is such a position intended for Arab ears alone? I'm not sure. After answering an initial question from me, the Three Faiths Forum cut off communication when I asked why the venom-tongued Tantawi would be an acceptable patron. Regardless, his is not the God of novelty but of duplicity. I, for one, am not sufficiently Christian to "turn the other cheek." Reformers of Islam should do battle with duplicity in order to actually accomplish something. That demands going beyond interfaith dialogue.

I CAN ENVISION A WORLD OF INTERFAITH *DIRECT ACTION.* FIRST on the action list, we need a take-no-prisoners debate about Saudi Arabia, a cauldron of duplicity. That debate should take place on university campuses, where students and professors already line up to dissect Israel—but let the Saudis get away with silky-smooth doublespeak. The World Assembly of Muslim Youth (WAMY), an organization bankrolled by the Saudis, distributes pamphlets on various North American campuses. One flyer, titled "Human Rights in Islam," coos about all that an Islamic state allows, implying that just because you *can* have "the right to protest against tyranny," you *do* have this right. The brochure sings the praises of fourteen freedoms, such as "protection from arbitrary imprisonment." But if you're deliberately targeted as a Shia Muslim, then you haven't been *arbitrarily* imprisoned, have you? As I've shown, Saudi Arabia harms Shia Muslims with no compunction.

Let's explore another of the brochure's celebrated freedoms— "equality before the law." However, if the law itself allows discrimination based on belief or biology, then that's what defines "equality." And so it is in Saudi Arabia, where the law prevents a woman from managing any business she owns, and where women are minors—which means even if Riyadh magically announced that all Saudi adults could vote, it would still be a right exclusively for men. Finally, read what WAMY itself says about women: "It is not permissible to oppress women. . . . Women's honor and chastity are to be respected under all circumstances." Wait a second. The obsession with honor in and of itself oppresses. What we're really reading, then, is a self-justifying abuse of dignity. These sleights of hand seep into "freedom of conscience and conviction" as well as "protection of religious sentiments"—two more liberties flaunted by WAMY and flouted by desert Islam. To those students and professors who fancy themselves critical thinkers because they can go toe-to-toe with Zionists, I have a challenge for you: Take on Saudi mouthpieces, who are nothing if not masters of hermetically sealed logic.

For the hardier souls among Christian, Jewish, and Muslim university students, interfaith direct action could mean organizing an "Abrahamic hajj" to Mecca. Abraham was not only the progenitor of these faiths; fittingly, according to Islam, he was the prophet who (with his son Ishmael) renovated the Kaaba— that black cube around which a large part of the hajj literally revolves. It's here that Prophet Muhammad reportedly smashed the idols of pagan Mecca, although he salvaged a crucifix from the residue. Only Muslims may pray at the Kaaba, you say? Then what's a Muslim? I eavesdropped on an online interfaith conversation recently and discovered openness to that question. A chatter named Aasim said to another chatter called Mattcabe, "Though you, as a Jew, are not a Muslim in the sense of practicing Islam as a formal way of life, I would consider you a muslim in the sense of giving yourself to God and having the desire to follow His commands. So, perhaps the idea that I am closer to Judaism and you are closer to Islam because of our belief in the One God revealed to Abraham isn't so far off the mark!" Such discussions, which an Abrahamic hajj would inspire, can bring a universal spirit to Mecca—a globalism that graces Jerusalem, Rome, and Geneva (the spiritual womb of Protestantism). If Mecca is too special to be pollinated by the presence of non-Muslims, I have only one question: Why?

However the Saudis react to an Abrahamic hajj, they'll eventually need to be honest. Agreeing to it while holding up visas forever—a favored gimmick that permits the kingdom to keep the curtains drawn on itself—simply won't wash. They'll be called on their deceit, over and over again. University students would do the calling, having fine-tuned their b.s. detectors through campus debates about Saudi Arabia.

I'll go one better: In planning the Abrahamic hajj, North American students ought to connect with Iranian students. An astonishing proportion of Iranian youth are intellectual renegades. Far from being a sea of "Down with America" messages, their banners often declare, "Down with Monopoly" (by which they mean the clerical monopoly on morality). Young Iranians listen to Israeli radio for balance and a high rate of Internet access makes them more wired to the outside world than other Muslims. Also, being Shias, they don't feel the need to legitimize the Sunni overlords of Saudi Arabia. That's not to say Iran's ayatollahs don't traffic in Saudi-style terror. Many do, and Hezbollah thanks them, I'm sure. Yet they're the ayatollahs against whom Iran's students are mounting a mighty, and largely nonviolent, rebellion.

In fact, it was a twenty-nine-year-old friend in Iran who e-mailed me Martin Luther King Jr.'s "Letter from Birmingham Jail." I'd never read it before. My friend prefaced it with this sentiment: When your broad-minded buddies in North America hesitate to expose Saudi Arabia for fear of offending Muslims, remind them of the Birmingham liberals who wanted King to stop fomenting needless tension in their town. King told them, "I must confess that I am not afraid of the word 'tension.' I have earnestly opposed violent tension, but there is a type of con-structive, nonviolent tension which is necessary for growth. Just as Socrates felt that it was necessary to create a tension in the mind so that individuals could rise from the bondage of myths and half-truths to the unfettered realm of creative analysis and objective appraisal, we must see the need for nonviolent gadflies to create the kind of tension in society that will help men rise from the dark depths of prejudice and racism to the majestic heights of understanding and brotherhood." I pray that Opera-tion Ijtihad will have such an effect.

Behold, then, a few of Operation Ijtihad's "bombs"—basic, bold questions that will have to be posed publicly:

- In debates about women's empowerment: Can a God that's deployed as ammunition against half His worshipers be truly loved? Does love matter?
- In discussions about media: Can the availability of books help rein in the hollow gods of materialism and fluff TV?

Why, over the past one thousand years, has the entire Arab world translated only as many books as Spain translates every year? Is it because the more people know about foreign notions, the more likely they'll be to examine their own? On the flip side, why isn't Egypt flooding Western markets with English translations of Gaber Asfour's *Against Fanaticism* or Ali Salem's *A Drive to Israel,* each of which showcases the potential for tolerance among Muslims? Has every last Western publisher rejected these manuscripts?

• In talks with Saudi Arabia over an Abrahamic hajj: Why do the Saudis outlaw Christian activity on their soil while financing a Center for Muslim-Christian Understanding in Washington, D.C.? Who, exactly, needs this "understanding"? What lessons from the center have the Saudis applied at home?

I'm not saying that such bombs will dismantle autocracies in one fell swoop. What I'm rooting for is a long-term cumulative result. When government ineptness and underfunded public services are criticized by taxpaying women who expect accountability for their money, and when intentional discrimination against women, religious minorities, and assorted "others" is dragged into broad daylight by the rising courage to ask questions aloud, Muslims will inevitably be better prepared for the transition to democracy.

I pray for a final result: that over time Operation Ijtihad will embolden the international community to spot and stop the origins of genocide—origins that might be associated with religion. Until we thoroughly investigate, we won't know the extent to which Wahhabi doctrine has laid the seedbed for ethnic or sectarian violence in Arab-occupied Sudan, where Osama bin Laden hung out before packing off to Afghanistan. But we do know enough to investigate. Two million people have been killed in Sudan, reports Charles Jacobs of the American Anti-Slavery Group. "Tens of thousands have been displaced, and 100,000 . . . forcibly starved." Why do these travesties go on? Why do we let them?

To date, no international agency has been purged of its dysfunction and invested with the clarity of justice so that massive hate crimes can be averted. The United Nations wasn't willing to preempt genocide in Rwanda. Given that the UN operates on protocol more than on principle, with jackboot regimes treated as morally equivalent to democracies, would the UN embarrass Saudi Arabia with an inquiry into Wahhabism? Hardly. As for the newly established International Criminal Court, it's meant to be reactive rather than proactive. Anyway, as of spring 2003, the court faced two hundred complaints about crimes against humanity. Why would it appoint a prosecutor to probe Wahhabism when neither the United States nor Saudi Arabia has signed on to the ICC?

Right now, our best bet for intercepting religiously motivated homicides might be to use the justice system in our own countries. As I write this, Britain's criminal courts have successfully prosecuted a Saudi-trained, London-based cleric for soliciting the murder of Jews, Hindus, and Americans. It's the first such conviction in England. It ought not to be the last.

I recognize that complaining to the courts sometimes has the feel of weapons-grade whininess. In France, as I mentioned at the top of this open letter, four Muslim groups tried to sue writer Michel Houellebecq because he told a literary magazine that Islam is "the most stupid" religion. "When you read the Koran, you give up. The Bible, at least, is beautiful because the Jews have a sublime literary talent." To the relief of anybody with an opinion about anything, the judge eventually dismissed this case. Italian journalist Oriana Fallaci went through a similar fight for free expression after the release of her pungent essay, *The Rage and the Pride.* In it, she kicks sand in the face of Muslim immigrants ("They breed too much") and their European hosts ("Italians don't produce babies anymore, the idiots"). The court case against her went nowhere.

By proposing criminal charges against the Saudis, am I merely mimicking those who would shut down Houellebecq, Fallaci, Nasrin, and Rushdie? God, I hope not. Challenging the Saudis isn't about shutting down Islam but letting more than strain bloom in the desert. And challenging them could help prevent another round of mass extermination while protecting many a nation's security. How the Koran is allowed to be interpreted—and how it isn't—has become everybody's business.

THERE WOULD BE A STRATEGIC SPIN-OFF TO OPERATION IJTIHAD, both for America and for key European nations. In pursuing it together, they'd go far toward healing the gulf between them. "Yes to the market economy, no to the market society!" thunders Lionel Jospin, France's former prime minister. Operation Ijtihad will lend itself to the balance between market and society. By ennobling Muslim women as micro-entrepreneurs, it would endorse the small-is-beautiful ethic of those who oppose corporate culture. Operation Ijtihad would focus on local people, not on industrial behemoths, thereby distinguishing between need and greed. And it would give Muslims a future to live for rather than a past to die for. Wouldn't these motives comfort fervent leftists within the European Union? The fact that many of them hate capitalism ought to be immaterial. Why should ideological aristocrats steal opportunity from Muslims? Doesn't such selfishness amount to neocolonialism, elevating the wishes of a distant elite over the welfare of millions of human beings? At least the stodgy World Bank appears to buy into the aims of Operation Ijtihad. When he was its chief economist, Nicholas Stern said, "Increasing gender equality is central to the idea of development as freedom." When women get involved, "[t]he evidence shows that education, health, productivity, credit and governance work better." In short, there's less corruption.

Women in the Islamic world, Western governments, free-thinking Muslims, Jews and Christians of goodwill, students, social activists, the World Bank, Oprah: Operation Ijtihad could be multifaceted. To be unremitting, though, it will need the resources of America. Enter the politics of oil.

A lot of us swear up, down, and sideways that Washington soft-pedals democracy in the Arab Muslim world simply to safe-guard America's oil supply. Even if that's true, oil doesn't *have* to stymie U.S. support for Operation Ijtihad. Not as long as America continues to tap a good deal more energy from outside the Middle East than within it, and not as long as alternative fuel sources exist aplenty. Of course, there's more to the realpolitik of oil. There's the dilemma of "Riyadh-politik."

What I mean is that Washington is in a double bind. On the one hand, dramatically choking off Saudi oil revenues would torpedo the king's authority as dispenser of stipends and other perks to clerics. If that pact collapses overnight, radical mullahs who already froth against the West will be given a dangerous triumph—and an excuse to become that much more radical. On the other hand, Washington has to help irrigate the desert with ideas and economic activity, even if it does so incrementally. Failing to act can only threaten future Americans, along with unsung others, as Saudi Arabia's oil reserves dry up. And drying up they are: Since the 1980s, per capita income in the kingdom has plunged from $23,000 to $7,000. For the privilege of cleaning dishes in Saudi Arabia, Bangladeshi Muslims pay Riyadh $2,000 (four-fifths of a first year's salary), topping up dwindling government coffers. Many Saudi youth won't touch manual work, yet their intellectual skills don't keep pace because their schools remain poached in religious studies. Artificially dependent on fossil fuels, Saudi Arabia's society can no longer afford to be fossilized. America can't afford this, either. Once launched, Operation Ijtihad could diversify the Saudi economy so that everyone gains in dignity, security, and independence. That includes women, whose needed entrepreneurship will shake desert Islam at its core.

Saudi Arabia doesn't have to be the starting point for Operation Ijtihad. In the name of moving incrementally, postwar Iraq can be. Historically, Iraqis have achieved among the highest literacy rates in the Middle East. Historically, too, this region has accepted women's participation in society. But drafting a constitution and holding elections won't be enough to spur a peaceful revival of cultural and economic pride. Generating wealth is crucial to sustaining any new democracy because only a business class that can be taxed by the state will, in turn, compel the state to develop institutions that respond to people.

Bear in mind something more: The Nazi pestilence spread, at first, through free elections. Adolf Hitler preyed on Germany's feelings of humiliation, reinforced by postwar economic devastation. We can't let Iraq reach that point. It easily can. Never mind that the Baath Party took the Nazi Party as its model; I'm more haunted by a photo that ran on the front page of *DAWN,* the Pakistani newspaper, during the lead-up to Operation Iraqi Freedom. The photo showed a group of grinning Palestinian women tearing a white rabbit to shreds as part of their training in defense of Iraq and of Islam, blood literally on their hands. What women can accomplish will be infinitely more constructive if Operation Ijtihad sees the light of day.

Meanwhile, one more group is poised to demonstrate the possibilities of reforming Islam: Muslims in the West. We have the luxury of exercising civil liberties, especially free expression, to change tribal tendencies. Are we leveraging that freedom? Are enough non-Muslims challenging us to do so?

8

IN PRAISE OF HONESTY

"I remember receiving enormous numbers of very moving letters from Muslim readers of *The Satanic Verses,*" Salman Rushdie told me during an interview in 2002. "Particularly from Muslim women, who thanked me for opening a door, you know." Boy, do I know. A week earlier, women had organized a conference of Toronto-area Muslims hungry for reform. Most of the female participants weren't wearing the hijab, not even a fetching version of it. Yet they cared enough about Islam to turn out on a gorgeous Saturday morning to discuss what's coming next for the faith—and their place in it.

A seditious figure stood at the podium. "Why do I need thirty thousand books in my library? Is it because every single book says exactly the same thing?" wondered Khaled Abou El Fadl, the UCLA professor who adopted stray dogs to defy mean-spirited Muslims. "The way we Muslims treat our intellectual heritage is very much as if book after book should affirm the 'simple truth' that is Islam and we need not go beyond."

Today's Muslim scholars "must be the most dull, the most bor-
ing products that humanity has known. Because each one of
them can say, 'What I'm going to do with my life is I'm going to
write exactly the same things that were said for the past six hundred years.' "

The crowd chuckled. En route to an empty chair, I nodded
to a gay Muslim friend who was dating a kippa-topped Jewish
boy. Before taking my seat, I exchanged embraces with a Bosnian Turk whom I hadn't seen since she married a Mexican raised
as a Catholic. They're now part of a Sufi Muslim circle in Mex-
ico City. This was an audience unlikely to eject El Fadl any time
soon.

He relished the love-in and went for broke. "Have you ever
known a civilization that grows on the basis of the lowest common denominator? A civilization that can be secure in the hands
of its simpletons rather than its geniuses? Civilization is built by
the artist, by the literary exponent, by the ability to generate
beauty and music and new methods of expression. Civilization
advances when there's a premium, not a fatwa, on originality of
thought!" I wanted to start a wave, but with everybody else rapt,
I smothered the impulse in an "inner jihad" sort of way.

Just one thing needled me. If El Fadl's fighting words had
come from a non-Muslim, the speaker's metaphorical neck
would have been wrung—not by militants (who don't bother
with metaphors) but by most of the moderates in the room.
Now, there's nothing specifically Muslim about this. When
African-American comedian Chris Rock can pepper his act
with the word "nigger" but Jennifer Lopez, a Latina, raises hack-
les for rapping the same word with no pejorative intent, Muslims aren't the only ones preoccupied with the politics of
"representing." But why can't proper representation depend on

shared values rather than the superficial similarities of skin color for blacks, sexual orientation for gays, religion for Muslims? I imagine that most of the women listening to El Fadl that day would make mincemeat of anyone who ordered them to wear a girdle over their dresses. Why, then, would any of us want to impose corsets of correctness on non-Muslims?

Or are non-Muslims censoring themselves?

I had reason to ponder that question a few days before El Fadl's appearance. A friend (let's call him Alex) was decorating the University of Toronto's student center with signs that featured fingers pointing up and down to orient newcomers. Having designed these signs on his computer, Alex took pride in showcasing that he'd made the fingers nonwhite. In one sign, the finger was black; in the other, gray (the closest his printer could get to brown). When Alex showed me these signs, I smiled in support. Then Alex mentioned an article in the newspaper that day about Islamic extremism in Denmark. "Stereotyping all Muslims," he chided the newspaper.

Having read the article, I disagreed with Alex. "I think they're bringing really troubling stuff to light," I said. Instantaneously, he seconded my dismay that some Muslims are abusing Denmark's liberalism, and that mainstream silence pardons their behavior. He recalled a statistic in the article: Even though Muslims make up only 5 percent of Denmark's population, they consume 40 percent of its welfare handouts. Worrying, because when the state pays troublemakers to live, they can buy the time to organize and execute their plans. I can't tell you if the statistic is accurate, but it clearly disturbed Alex. Yet, in his desire not to offend the Muslim in me, he'd first accused the paper of journalistic malfeasance. Alex's "harmless" dishonesty matched that of countless Muslims.

If you're an Alex, please listen. There's more than one way to exploit Islam. Some Muslims exploit it as a sword, and they're goons for doing so. But just as many—or more—Muslims exploit Islam as a shield, and that's destructive, too. It protects Muslims from self-inquiry and non-Muslims from guilt. "You have no right to question my religion," the shield-wavers often sermonize to non-Muslims. "You'll never understand Islam." (Among the multiple meanings of this statement: *I,* as an insecure Muslim, don't want to understand where *you're* coming from.) "You've 'racialized' my people in the past and you'll 'problematize' us again." (Subtext: We Muslims have no power of our own. That's what my cultural studies professor taught me.)

I've watched this ploy too many times to be delicate in describing it. So I'll just tell it like it is: Since my young adulthood, Muslims in the West have been sucking on the nipple of public ignorance about Islam, wailing for validation under all conditions, at all costs. Other commentators have noticed. Even before September 11, British journalist Yasmin Alibhai-Brown wrote that the "idea of our society as simply a non-interference pact between groups is not just wrong, it is impossible. We are all now necessarily involved with each other." We've got to lay down the shield and accept the birthright of any open society: that we can ask questions of each other. Sometimes pointed questions. Sometimes in public.

In this spirit, we shouldn't let multicultural bromides anes-thetize our brains any further. But that's what we're doing. For example, a project called Muslims in the American Public Square lauds the Joseph's coat that is the U.S. Muslim con-stituency. "[A]lphabetically our membership ranges from Alba-nians, Afghans and Algerians at one end to Yemenis and Zanzibar on the other," toots the project's website. "What is comforting to some of us is the fact that here in the United States . . . a new sense of Muslim solidarity is in the making." Old divisions dissolving, unity arising from diversity. Muslims in the American Public Square present the classic coming-of-age story.

Except for one glitch: At last check, no woman sat on its advisory board. Moreover, the project posted a photo of twenty-five "national Muslim leaders" who came together for a focus group it organized, and there wasn't a woman among them. I don't care about equal numbers for the sake of equal numbers. My complaint has to do with essential steps not being taken to chip away at tribal Islam. Given the contemporary Muslim world's abysmal record on human rights, which include women's rights, here's my equation: No women equals not enough pluralism and not enough change. Has anyone alerted these Muslims in the American Public Square to the cavernous hole in their "diversity," or would doing so upset the multi-culti joviality of their jamborees?

I want to offer another, longer-standing, example of how we in the West are being tranquilized by multiculturalism's vibe. In 1994, the deputy prime minister of Malaysia, Anwar Ibrahim, gave a talk at Georgetown University called "The Need for Civilizational Dialogue." Anwar admitted that "[i]gnorance, injustice, corruption, hypocrisy and the erosion in moral rectitude are quite prevalent in contemporary Muslim societies." However, he warned, "The gullible consumer of the mass media of today would form the impression that the Muslim world is only populated by stern and menacing fundamentalists." The fact is, Muslim civilization "has produced plenty of love stories." Anwar illustrated this point with "the enchanting tale" of Laila and Majnun. "As the story goes, the young man was scorned and ridiculed for his obsession with the maiden, because to the eyes of the world Laila was hideous in physical appearance. In response to this, the youth always replied: 'To see the beauty of Laila, one requires the eyes of Majnun.'" Aww, repulsive Laila found love—how uplifting.

At the risk of ruining the romance of this moment, I must ask: Does Laila have the choice to stay single rather than marry Majnun? May she exit the country without his okay? Can she choose her career? Can she have a career? Was any one of these questions asked aloud by the non-Muslims who attended the speech? Anwar Ibrahim wouldn't have melted under the interrogation. He wants human rights, and that's what alarmed his boss, Malaysia's prime minister, who later threw him in prison to shut him up. Why be polite about pretty stories that might bespeak ugly realities?

NOTE TO NON-MUSLIMS: DARE TO RUIN THE ROMANCE OF THE moment. Open societies remain open because people take the risk of asking questions—out loud. Questions like, "Why is it so easy to draw thousands of Muslims into the streets to denounce France's ban on the hijab, but impossible to draw even a fraction of those demonstrators into the streets to protest Saudi Arabia's *imposition* of the hijab?" And when Muslims insist, "We're democracies in our own way," they need to hear this question posed: "What rights do women and religious minorities exercise in such democracies—not in theory, but in actuality?"

No doubt, among the responses you'll get is that the West should take a hard look at how it's mutilating women through breast implants and tummy tucks for the sake of social acceptance. Agreed, the West should look hard. Still, in all my years as a feminist in the West, I've never met a girl whose parents have disowned her because she wouldn't inject silicon into her boobs—and yet more than a few Muslim parents have rejected their daughters for resisting clitoral circumcision. Non-Muslims do the world no favors by pushing the moral mute button as soon as Muslims start speaking. Dare to ruin the moment.

Ask the self-styled thinkers of our times—peace activists, for instance—why they make alliances with certain characters and expect the rest of us to clap. In January 2003, as the UN Security Council debated how to disarm Saddam Hussein, I observed Toronto's antiwar protest. The final speaker of the day—the anchor of the antiwar dream team, if you will—publishes a newspaper that valorizes Iranian-style theocracy. I had to wonder whether the hooting, whistling, cheering masses would even have the legal right to gather if guys like him got their way. That same afternoon in Washington, D.C., antiwar organizers gave the stage to a Muslim cleric who, in October 2001, opined that "the Zionists in Hollywood, the Zionists in New York, and the Zionists in D.C." are colluding against Muslims. If the United States needs to reconsider its alliances, progressive Westerners need to do likewise. But you won't know how tawdry some partner-ships are until you dare to ruin the moment and ask.

Ask about the money you give to charity. According to Women Living under Muslim Laws, any number of "donor agencies" unwittingly finance madressas and social work offices run by foundamentalists. The foundamentalists, in turn, exacer-bate "pressure for the men to attend mosques [and] for women to cover themselves." They push "the end of coeducational schooling, the banning of girls from sciences, sports and arts, [and] educational programmes that promote a hatred of others."

Don't be hoodwinked by seemingly neutral titles, either. The Benevolence International Foundation, the Mercy International Relief Organization, the Global Relief Foundation—all are soothing names, and all are implicated in Islamic terror. Then there's Human Concern International, a Muslim charity based in Ottawa. For some time, its regional director for Pakistan, a Canadian citizen named Ahmed Said Khadr, sweet-talked other Muslim Canadians into handing over jewelry and checks to "alleviate human suffering." Apparently, they had no whiff that he might be a senior Al-Qaeda operative. After Pakistani authorities arrested Khadr in a bomb plot in 1995, Human Concern fired him. Once released, Khadr started a rival charity under the equally pacific banner, Health and Education Projects International. I'm not urging you to stop giving. I'm urging you to stop taking for granted where your donations go. Dare to ruin the moment.

You're comfortable with putting politicians on the hot seat, right? Not quite as scary as calling Muslims to account, is it? Okay. If you're an American citizen, how do you know your tax dollars aren't funding belligerent textbooks in Afghanistan, as they did during the Reagan era under the U.S. Agency for International Development? Have you pumped your member of Congress for information? If you live in Norway, are you aware that English-language training schools run by your state (paid for by you) sometimes segregate Muslim women from Muslim men, thereby failing to introduce these immigrants to a basic tenet of pluralism—coeducation? To the residents of Holland, how are you ensuring that the Dutch Muslim Broadcasting System no longer supplies hate-dipped content to your public TV station, Nederland 1, as it did on September 11, 2001? To the people of Canada, you should know that on the first anniversary of September 11 a federally funded group, Toronto Response for Youth (TRY), held workshops about the need for tolerance. But TRY's material attributed the media's stereotypes of Muslims and others to "corporations run by mostly Caucasian or Jewish males." This is *anti*racism? For whom? Alice and Ali in Wonderland? Can we *try* to spend our money on more honest endeavors?

Some of you may be grumbling to yourselves, "But it's true that white guys and Jews head all the media-owning multinationals. Does telling the truth make us racists?" Putting aside a black man named Richard Parsons, CEO of AOL–Time Warner, and Oprah Winfrey, and Sonny Mehta and Quincy Jones, let's suppose you're right that whites and Jews command mainstream culture. As long as we're playing on those terms, it behooves me to divulge something more about TRY, the "antiracism" project. Most of the workshop leaders had Muslim names. Maybe we shouldn't be surprised that antiracism takes the form of anti-Semitism when Muslims mind the store. Or does my "profiling" of these individuals make me a racist? Aren't the "antiracists" also profiling by envisaging pale skins and yarmulkes behind media stereotypes? Are they more, less, or simply as racist as I am? You can see how tedious such a contest becomes.

Far more worthwhile is to ask why the legitimate questioning of some people (Muslims, for instance) carries the charge of being racist while the legitimate questioning of other people (say, non-Muslim Americans) doesn't. After all, neither America nor Islam is monochromatic. Neither is a "race" in the fatuous genetic sense. So what gives? At least three things.

First, Americans think of themselves as being defined by an idea—freedom. Although their country isn't color-blind, the idea of freedom is. In part, that's why it wouldn't make sense to call inquisitors of America "racists." Because the devastating accusation of racism doesn't get slung at critics of America, their criticism strikes us as permissible. And it *is* permissible—just as criticism of the demographically diverse Islamic nation ought to be. Muslims who automatically allege racism against interrogators of Islam are themselves cementing the fiction that we all come from one place. You can't blame that stereotype on Jews or white men.

There's a second reason that it feels like fair ball to question non-Muslim Americans—and Westerners in general—but not Muslims. People of the West don't make a habit of physically damaging you for dissenting with officialdom. Not every American welcomes the fact that the *New York Times Magazine* skewered the FBI's estimated number of Al-Qaeda recruits in America, calling it "more or less a wild guess." But, were the magazine's offices set ablaze, as happened in Nigeria when a columnist inadvertently ticked off the ruling Muslims? Various American cable channels have broadcast commercials that ask, "What would Jesus drive?" thereby pricking the oil oligarchy. These channels also aired Nelson Mandela's indictment of George W. Bush "as a president who can't think properly." But were their licenses revoked or their journalists roughed up? By way of comparison, Saudi Arabia, Kuwait, and Jordan have expelled Al-Jazeera reporters for criticizing their regimes.

It's a testament to how much self-criticism the United States tolerates that after September 11, Jello Biafra, front man for the 1980s punk band Dead Kennedys, toured North American cities with a rant about Bush. Biafra ridiculed Bush's twang while delivering grammatically garbled statements made by the president, to the gob-smacked delight of his audiences.

God Himself is up for teasing in some regions of the United

States. I once watched a man in Venice Beach, California, belt out his own rendition of "God Bless America." Enjoy:

> *God bless my underpants!*
> *Brand that I like*
> *Stand inside them*
> *And ride them*
> *Between my buns when I ride or I bike . . .*

Our man may be a goofball, but his briefs didn't get inspected by irate FBI agents or his buns kicked by Christian evangelists. Try warbling something about Allah in a Muslim country. We already know the hysteria that breaks out when Prophet Muhammad is quipped about—and he's not even God!

Returning to America, let me say that the president's men do swoop in where they can. Arbitrary arrests, random searches, unwarranted seizures, tapped phones, opened mail, classified government documents: The United States sees it all. Soldiers at a military base in California may shoot to kill if antiwar activists trespass. The Pentagon has an entertainment liaison office that cuts deals with Hollywood to sanitize depictions of the U.S. military at the expense of historical accuracy. The state of Florida, governed by George W. Bush's little brother, Jeb, recently ordered a driver to turn in his license plate because it read "ATHEIST." And Texas-based Clear Channel, America's biggest radio network as well as a financial booster of the president, has lent support to the war on terror by shelving almost 160 tunes that could affront post–September 11 sensibilities. Uh huh, policing abounds in the land of the free.

But so does the daily documenting of it. You and I know about America's inanities because we hear about them incessantly.

It's natural to lambaste a country when we're aware of its blemishes, and it's natural to publicize those blemishes when we know we won't get our tongues, arms, or heads lopped off. Muslims should wonder if such luxuries (known in the West as "rights") contribute to why we casually dump on America and Israel to the exclusion of examining Islamic countries. Non-Muslims should wonder why they don't ask us that question more often.

Now for a final reason that we consider it civil to criticize Americans but not Muslims. Not only will the United States listen to an itemizing of its failures, the United States will take responsibility for a few of them. Even when it comes to that most sacrosanct of religions, money, Americans will sometimes engage in transparent introspection to set things right. Throughout the summer of 2002, CNBC, the finance channel of choice in the United States, covered the accounting swindles at the mammoth energy company Enron. "What Went Wrong?" beamed one of CNBC's graphics. Six months later, *Time* magazine named its Persons of the Year: the whistleblowers of corporate America. All were women. All had a legal, judicial, and political system to turn to that apparently cared about what they had to say. Where in the Muslim world would you find women being hailed for busting corruption? Nowhere. Not yet.

It's up to us in the West to drop reactionary charges of racism against the whistleblowers of Islam and lead the charge for change.

INSTIGATING CHANGE MEANS NOT TAKING THE KORAN LITERALLY, and also not taking multiculturalism literally. Why should forced clitorectomy be indulged? Why should the cops back off when a father (or mother) threatens death to a daughter who chooses to marry outside the religion? Why should a Muslim cabbie who rapes a mentally disabled woman get off under the rubric of cultural sensitivity? To echo the German political science professor and practicing Muslim, Bassam Tibi, why should human rights *belong* to non-Muslims?

As Westerners bow down before multiculturalism, we often act as if anything goes. We see our readiness to accommodate as a strength—even a form of cultural superiority (though few of us will admit that). But foundamentalists see our inclusive instincts as a weakness that makes us soft, lardy, rudderless. Foundamentalists detest weakness. They believe the weak deserve to be vanquished. Paradoxically, then, the more we accommodate to placate, the more their contempt for our "weakness" grows. The ultimate paradox may be that in order to defend our diversity, we'll need to be less tolerant. At the very least, we'll need to be more vigilant.

Vigilance requires asking a spiritual (but not necessarily religious) question: What guiding value can most of us live with? From the panoply of ideologies and faiths out there, what filter will distill almost everybody's right to free expression? A watery word like *tolerance* or a slippery phrase like *mutual respect* won't cut it as a guiding value. Why tolerate violence-bent bigotry? Where's the *mutual* in this version of *mutual respect?* Amin Maalouf, a novelist in France, nails the point: "Traditions deserve to be respected only insofar as they are respectable—that is, exactly insofar as they themselves respect the fundamental rights of men and women." We, Muslim and non-Muslim Westerners, need to decide on a value that reflects this sensibility and work backwards from there. Whatever doesn't move society in the direction of that value shouldn't be tolerated. Full stop.

Such a dragnet will catch certain interpretations of Islam, and so be it. I'm about to invoke a sensational yet genuine example of what can't be tolerated if we're going to maintain freedom of expression for as many people as possible. In 1999, the self-appointed "Sharia Court of the UK" issued a death warrant against playwright Terence McNally. His show, *Corpus Christi,* portrayed Jesus as a gay man. Exercising the right to free expression, many a Christian picketed *Corpus Christi* at its Edinburgh debut. Sheikh Omar bin Bakri Muhammad, a judge of the Sharia Court, went further by playing the honor card. Scolding the Church of England for "neglect[ing] the honour of the Virgin Mary and Jesus," Sheikh Omar signed a fatwa against McNally, then had it distributed in London. Freedom of expression? In a manner of speaking. If carried out, however, the fatwa would cut short McNally's life, expunging and not merely reducing his freedom of expression.

To be perfectly fair, the fatwa stressed that McNally should only be executed in an Islamic state. And it did give him an out: By converting to Islam, the playwright could escape the beheading. A half-measure, such as repentance, wouldn't lift his death sentence, but "his family would be cared for by the Islamic state carrying out the sentence and he could be buried in a Muslim graveyard." Oh, rapture.

Tell me one good reason why Sheikh Omar should have been allowed to remain in Britain after counseling a man's death. The Muslim Council of Britain claims that Sheikh Omar represents no more than a thousand Muslims out of the country's 2 million. If that's true, then British Muslims—indeed, Muslims throughout the West—don't need to fret over his prosecution or deportation because all forms of Islam that respect the freedom to disbelieve, to go one's own way, will endure. Only desert

Islam won't, and shouldn't we all breathe a sigh of relief at that prospect?

I propose that, as a guiding value, we in the West agree on individuality. When we celebrate individuality, we let *most* people choose who they are, be they members of a religion, free spirits, or both. For a lot of Europeans, individuality might ring too much of American individualism. It doesn't have to. Individualism—*I'm out for myself*—differs from individuality—*I'm myself, and my society benefits from that uniqueness.* My question to non-Muslim Europe is this: Do you believe that your 16 million Muslims are capable of contributing as individuals? The question is not whether they're capable, but whether you believe they are.

Europe, why do you hesitate to imagine Muslims as full citizens? Many Muslim families have lived in Germany since the Second World War. Why are they still referred to as second- and third-generation immigrants instead of as Germans? What's with the purity hang-up—something you claim to abhor about Israel, even though Israel has long conferred citizenship on foreigners? I plead with you, Europe, not to conjure an unholy alliance between desert tribalism and your own tribalisms. Let down your defenses and learn from the North American pluralistic model, in which Muslims can become integrated citizens. Do you want to see pluralism retrench because, that way, America will retrench with it? Sure, you'll spite Americans, but you'll also be impugning your liberal forebears, from Averroes to Erasmus to Kant to Voltaire. (And Voltaire, let's be frank, would have raised a glass to the coarse Yank who sang "God Bless My Underpants.")

Europe, have you resigned yourselves to the rumor that your time is past and therefore you have no stake in the future? You went ballistic over the latest American war in Iraq, but immigration from Muslim lands should be an equally galvanizing issue for you. Your survival as a distinct economic bloc relies on immigrants at least as much as North America's future does. You've got an enlightened self-interest in helping Arab Muslims adapt to democracy before they descend in greater numbers on your cities. So why aren't you rallying against Arab regimes in which Sunni Muslim minorities control the Shia majorities? Like many of you, I'm allergic to religious sectarianism. Nevertheless, where's your antipathy to apartheid in these cases?

What do you say to Rami Khouri, the Palestinian journalist who writes that "[i]ndependent, credible, civil society institutions are nonexistent in most of the Persian Gulf, Syria, Iraq, and Libya, and operate under heavy state controls in Sudan, Algeria, Tunisia, and Yemen"? Europe, your economies are struggling right now, and of course you should guard against the anti-Arab racism that economic malaise can spur. But be careful of the racism that comes from overcompensating. Depicting Zionists as European imperialists or Nazis isn't the way to redeem your afflicted consciences. Supporting human rights for all is. Who's preventing you from organizing colossal street demonstrations against the abuse of universal human freedoms?

Maybe you're tempted to tell me they're not universal. Maybe in your steely-eyed revolt against globalization—a process that supposedly standardizes lifestyles—you've concluded that the universality of freedoms is a slick euphemism for the uniformity of culture. Get real. Under globalization's "uniformity," nobody forces me on pain of execution to patronize the golden arches. I can choose *not* to read a McDonald's menu. I can choose to groove to the rhythms of Nusrat Fateh Ali Khan, to wear a T-shirt decrying sweatshop labor, and to board a train out of the country for one or another protest without first having to win my father's permission to travel. Under the uniformity of Islamic foundamentalism, I can't choose. Neither can you. Equating the evils of desert Islam with the sins of globalization is a mistake committed by the overprivileged, those who've never known anything worse than the horrors of being marketed to.

Europe, are you so smitten by the complexities of culture that you've lost sight of the certainties of civilization? There's a loaded word, civilization. But as I've shown, Muslims share in Western civilization. They acted as midwives to the European Renaissance, all the while employing Jews, Christians, and others, who, in turn, borrowed heavily from Greek, Byzantine, and surrounding traditions. Our global responsibility now is not to determine who owns what identity, but to convey to future generations what we all owe each other.

With this intent, I want to end where I started: in appreciation of what the West has done for me—indeed, for many Muslims. I owe the West my willingness to help reform Islam. In all honesty, my fellow Muslims, you do too.

---— 9 ———

THANK GOD
FOR THE WEST

It's Friday afternoon at the University of Toronto. Young Muslims are streaming out of the debates room at Hart House, the campus's Gothic-style student center. They've been praying in the very spot where prime ministers and presidents have refined arguments and traded witticisms. Framed pictures of world-famous visitors grace the walls. But you don't see those photos on most Friday afternoons because they're covered by squares of neatly sewn burlap. Hart House has installed sturdy wall hooks on both sides of every portrait so that canvas can be hung over the faces—a gesture of respect for those who wish to pray to God, not to God's creatures. One wonders whether the Taliban would have ever, under any circumstances, considered blanketing the historic Buddha statues instead of blowing them up. One also wonders whether the Muslim students know how good they've got it here.

By "here," I don't simply mean textured Toronto. Take Halifax. I would expect to glimpse only two types of get-ups there:

tartans worn by the male staff at tourist hotels and the military fatigues of soldiers stationed at the nearby base. While in Halifax one drizzly Friday, I spotted a man decked out in the full monty of a desert Arab: flowing white robe, headdress, sandals, even crooked stick as walking cane. Late for his Sabbath prayers, he was flagging down a taxi while talking on his cell phone. I interrupted him to ask the obvious. Ibrahim (yes, another one) told me that he dons his Islamic regalia every Friday. Been doing it for ten years. "Any harassment?" I probed. Not once. Quite the contrary: At Dalhousie University, where Ibrahim sells hot dogs, they affectionately call him the Dogfather.

Later, at the Halifax airport, a Muslim woman sat across from me in the lounge. She was clad in black, all the way to her leather gloves. Despite being busy, the lounge had no hurly-burly about it. People took the time to taste their coffee before swallowing. And yet, only I was checking out this woman. It wasn't that folks were trying not to appear invasive. It's just that nobody felt invaded by her. Before heading to the gate, she stood up and readjusted her chador. Still no stares. As she left the lounge, I saw a couple of heads lift, and then they went back to their crosswords.

Such stories are at odds with the highly hyped backlash against Muslims. I don't deny that since September 11, unprovoked anger has erupted at some "Arab-looking" people (among them, Israeli Jews). And those who have experienced a haranguing ought to speak up. I certainly contacted the media during the 1991 Gulf War, when a security guard marched me out of a government building for no stated reason. But what too seldom gets audited, quantified, and publicized is the opposite of "Islamophobia"— unsolicited eruptions of decency toward Muslims.

In North America, decency has erupted in spades. Immediately after September 11, Christian and Jewish clerics got in touch with Muslim leaders. They arranged multifaith services, press conferences, and fund-raising drives for any legal bills that Muslims might incur defending themselves against handcuff-happy authorities. On the very night of the terrorist attacks, when shock numbed most of us into silence, I received a phone call from one of Toronto's most prominent ministers. He wanted to know if I was safe and how he could help curb the hate I might now encounter. Over the next three days, more expressions of care came from my *Jewish* friends than from anybody else. My private conversations with young Muslims revealed much the same: teachers, neighbors, coworkers and chatroom users went out of their way to neutralize any narrow minds.

I tried to report these incidents of decency to the police, to an antiracism organization, to statistics crunchers, and to a national broadcaster. The first three had no idea what to do with my good news. It didn't fit their categories of collectibles. As for the broadcaster? My contact there—a Caucasian male, if it matters—replied that naming the decency could be viewed as a racist denial of the malice that plenty of Muslims were suffering. He asked, "What would we say to that?" Try this: If the nuances of Islam deserve to be recognized, so do the nuances of the West.

We're not mutually exclusive, Muslims and the West, and even America reassure us of that fact. Georgetown, a notable Jesuit university in Washington, D.C., has an imam. The U.S. armed forces have many. In October 2002, the U.S. Postal Service reissued a first-class stamp to commemorate Eid, the Muslim calendar's biggest party days. "This is a proud moment for the Postal Service, the Muslim community, and Americans in general," the *Arab News* quoted Azeezaly Jaffer as saying. Jaffer is vice-president of public affairs and communications for the

Postal Service. The Eid stamp may be bogus symbolism, but having a Muslim executive at a venerable American institution isn't.

The Islamic Society of North America attests to the mobility enjoyed by Muslims in this part of the world. "American Muslims as citizens have access to numerous educational and employment opportunities," the ISNA advertises. "These opportunities range from political appointments by the President of the United States to public service jobs and internships and fellowships in the White House and the State Department." Najeeb Halaby, father of Jordan's Queen Noor, headed the Federal Aviation Administration under President Kennedy. In her memoirs, Queen Noor points out that the president personally appealed to Halaby to take the position. What a contrast to the way Saudi Arabia treats its ethnic "outsiders."

How do dissidents of desert Islam, when exiled from their countries, end up earning a living? Many of the exiles teach and write freely at American colleges. "Is it hard to be an American Muslim today?" I asked my aunt. She lives in George W. Bush's home state of Texas.

"No," she shrugged. "Not if you have some confidence. Just don't go into hiding." On September 11, she was teaching at an Islamic school in Houston. I inquired about the community reaction the school faced. She talked of compassionate letters, calls, cards, and flowers sent by ordinary Texans. Her recollection jibes with what the *Los Angeles Times* heard from the Islamic Center of Southern California. "We are overwhelmed," said its religious director—and he meant overwhelmed with warmth. In the aftermath of September 11, a journalist friend dropped in on flag-clutching American farming towns and found similar concern for Muslims. "Someday," he later wrote me, "I hope someone will chronicle the great wave of openness and kindness and intelligence that emerged in America for about two months after the attacks." This friend has left-wing sympathies, and yet he, like me, doesn't understand why on God's green earth it would be racist to acknowledge civility.

The attribute I most rejoice in is curiosity. "I am a cynical person," said Muslim lobbyist Sarah Eltantawi to the *Los Angeles Times*. "But I am heartened by the earnestness and sincerity with which people are trying to learn about Islam." Following September 11, three editions of the Koran became best-sellers for amazon.com. The University of North Carolina made it mandatory for freshmen to read a book about the Koran. Although a lawsuit ensued, and flopped, an equally telling comment on American society came from UNC's twenty-one-year-old student body president. Said Jennifer Daum, "My feeling is that if you're not prepared to read ideas that are not your own and you might disagree with, you do not belong at an institution of higher learning."

This spirit of exploration is the oxygen for which I'm so grateful to North America. In much of the Muslim world, if you're more than you're assigned to be, you're considered less. In much of North America, Muslims have the freedom to be many-dimensional. All kinds of folks do. One New York casualty of September 11 was Father Mychal Judge, a gay Catholic priest mourned by the firefighters to whom he'd ministered for years. Pluralism of people, pluralism of ideas—draw the connection. I did, and that connection has so far saved my faith in Islam.

Had I grown up in a Muslim country, I'd probably be an atheist in my heart. It's because I live in this corner of the world, where I can think, dispute, and delve further into any topic, that I've learned why I shouldn't give up on Islam just yet.

After so much exploring, my personal interpretation of the Koran leads me to three recurring messages. First, only God knows fully the truth of anything. Second, God alone can punish unbelievers, which makes sense given that only God knows what true belief is. (And considering the Koran's mountain range of moods, it really would take the Almighty to know how it all hangs together.) Human beings must warn against corrupt practices, but that's all we can do to encourage piety. Third, our resulting humility sets us free to ponder God's will—without any obligation to toe a dictated line. "Let there be no compulsion in religion," states a voice in chapter 2 of the Koran. "Unto you your religion, unto me my religion," echoes another voice in chapter 109. In between, there's this: "If God had pleased, He would have made you all one people. But He has done otherwise . . ." Ain't that the truth.

My interpretation sheds light on why I, as a Muslim, can't stay quiet about Islam's supremacists, whether they're extreme like Osama bin Laden or mainstream like my madressa teacher, Mr. Khaki. After reaching their own conclusions "without compulsion," they turn around and prevent others from doing the same. At that point, the Koranically decreed duty to "warn" about practices that try the faith morphs into the Koranically denied permission to intimidate. By my reading, we should not only enjoy the freedom to explore, we have to ensure that this freedom exists for *everyone*. Anything less undermines God's jurisdiction as the supreme judge and jury. Such individual, independent reasoning is logical, potentially righteous, and entirely compatible with the ideals I hold as a Westerner.

I'm referring to pluralism, not consumerism. If you think Western ideals can only turn us into lazy fiends of the latest fads, tell me why I haven't shopped my way through spiritual anguish (except, in one case, to buy an English-language Koran). Instant gratification wouldn't have gratified me during the watershed moment when my boss asked me how I reconcile my Muslim faith to the flogging of a young, raped woman in Nigeria. As someone who treasures freedom of thought, I accepted his right to ask. Would you? Or would you have filed a harassment suit against him? Was he silencing me or signaling his faith in my ability to think this through? In taking up his challenge, was I a self-loathing crypto-imperialist or a partisan of the examined life? As a Muslim, how would I have grown if I'd insisted on my "right" to be free of reflection?

On to a question for the secular humanists among you. I respect your choice to take a leap into your own faith—nontheism—but what would I have gained by junking mine prematurely? Religion has supplied me with values (such as discipline) that compete with the materialism of life in North America. It's in this competition that I find an incentive to keep thinking. The tension between religion and secularism leads me to probe alternate truths and avoid lapsing into any fundamentalism of my own—be it feminist fundamentalism, nationalist fundamentalism, or multiculturalist fundamentalism. Religion has compelled me to bow to no one but the God dwelling restlessly in my conscience, a precious skill to develop in an era of boundless spin. Better, religion has taught me not to confuse authoritarianism with authority. You might stand to hear more about this, since those who incriminate all faith as "irrational" sometimes forget that rationality can become an orthodoxy unto itself.

Taslima Nasrin, who's a physician as well as a feminist, told me that "there is no afterlife. If you're dead, you're dead. Finished. Finito."

"From the purely scientific perspective, sure," I responded.

"But who's to say the scientific perspective is superior to any other perspective?"

"Because it's true."

"Aren't you fighting against orthodoxy?"

"I am fighting for truth. Devastated women seek shelter in religion and religion is for that. It's for weak people, vulnerable people, ignorant people, foolish people. But why should we be weak and vulnerable in the first place?"

"You know, Taslima, your critics can say that you're falling into the very pit that you claim they, as religious people, fall into. You're a *scientific* supremacist."

She laughed. "I'm not a scientific supremacist. I am for truth. Not big-T Truth, which is God's Truth, but small-t truth."

"But you don't believe in God."

After more sparring, her big-T Truth leaked out. "I want to abolish religion only because religion is against humanity. If religion is not against humanity, I have no problem with it." Well, that's reasonable enough.

Less reasonable is the assumption that religion must be relentlessly "against humanity." Michael Moore, America's most snide and vociferous proponent of people power, learned justice at the knee of Catholicism, says his close friend, Jeff Gibbs. According to Jimmy Carter, Israel's Menachim Begin and Egypt's Anwar Sadat clasped hands thanks in no small measure to their respective Jewish and Muslim values. A Hindu militant snuffed out the life of Mahatma Gandhi, yet Gandhi fashioned his earth-shaking concept of nonviolent resistance, or *satyagraha,* from Hinduism and Jainism. Come to think of it, I've never heard a committed secular humanist denounce the Dalai Lama for espousing religion—and here's a guy who inherited his position wholly through lineage!

The Dalai Lama, Martin Luther King Jr., Desmond Tutu, Malcolm X—they can be forgiven for "having religion" because of what they've done with religion. They've all sprung themselves—and their people—from the enfeebling patterns of victimhood. For Muslims worldwide, we in the West can be the harbingers of this transformation. We can do so not merely by condemning Islamo-fascists but by refusing to become Islamo-fetishists, those who stoke the Muslim inferiority complex by leaving the heavy lifting of change to somebody else. We need to depose our own victim mentality.

It won't be easy. I'll illustrate through another group of privileged "victims," middle-class African-Americans. In the summer of 2001, Michelle and I visited Atlanta, Georgia. On a Saturday we toured the Jimmy Carter Presidential Center, named for a leader who made civil rights the cornerstone of his domestic agenda. Save for me and a couple of workers, everyone at the Carter Center was white. Not one black visitor showed up during our three-hour stay. Next, we went to the tombstone of Martin Luther King, Jr., a landmark that brimmed with African-Americans and a few whites. I wondered how many people were going to the Carter Center, too. I made my inquiries.

Nobody expressed an interest in knowing about the Carter Center. One couple sniped, "Why would we waste our time at the shrine of a white man?" Um, because by paying tribute to Reverend King you're supposedly saluting the virtue of desegregation? And because it's not the color of a man's skin but the content of his character that was most prized by the visionary at whose grave you now snap your photos and strut your "free-at-last" swag?

I understand African-American frustration over the very notion of freedom. It's well founded. During my visit to Atlanta, the city's newspaper reported that several Georgia counties were paying a set fee to "contract lawyers." These lawyers existed not to defend their largely poor and black clientele, but to expedite their convictions so that the next batch of accused could be treated to the same backlog-clearing indignities. But most of those at the King memorial that day weren't materially malnourished. They flaunted their Nike Air Hyperflights, their state-of-the-art digicams, their SUVs. The people I spoke with seemed oblivious to their achievement of middle-class status—and to the president who helped them get there. More conversations revealed that they chose to be stuck in self-pity, like any number of Muslims in the West.

Muslims have to be extra cautious about passivity. Because of our outsized reliance on God, we too often minimize personal agency. *"Inshallah,"* we instinctively sigh. "If God wills." No. *We* must will. We've got to be God's partners in the journey to justice. "But who are we?" some of you might ask. After all, it's drilled into us that God is great!—*"Allahu Akbar!"* Only when I educated myself did I learn the actual meaning of this phrase— God is great*er*. Greater than His creatures, yes, but that's not a statement of our inconsequence. At bottom, the cry of "Allahu Akbar!" is a reminder to balance our agency with humility. I accept that I can't be a spiritual narcissist. Can the same be said of those who fling their fatwas against reason? And those of us who humor the fatwa-flingers?

DURING MY LIFETIME, TERRORISTS HAVE GONE FROM INFLICTING death tolls that number only a handful to hundreds, to thousands, to the possibility of hundreds of thousands. In roughly the same period, the Vatican has officially renounced anti-Semitism and martyrdom while contending more publicly than ever with sexual abuse of women and children, thanks to dissident Catholics. I've composed this open letter knowing both realities. A liberal Islamic reformation can take place—Muslims have no pope to persuade—but it's do or die. Silence is a nonstarter.

Yossi Klein Halevi, an Israeli journalist, a devout Jew, and a good friend, thinks I've been unduly harsh with you. "Islam is one of the world's great religions—that's not just a line," he reminds me. Yossi has written *At the Entrance to the Garden of Eden,* a book about his attempt to pray with Muslims and Christians in the Holy Land. Of all the Muslims he approached, only the Sufis welcomed him to bow beside them. It's everybody's loss that the Sufis are, by Yossi's own description, "absurdly peripheral" within Islam.

Still, he implores me to seek perspective. "Religions go through difficult periods. Think of the other two monotheistic faiths fourteen hundred years after their founding: Christianity in the age of inquisition and massacre, Judaism in the primitive age of the judges." But Islam's relative youth as a faith hardly absolves today's adult Muslims of our misdeeds—particularly our continued imitation of medieval misdeeds. Yossi himself tells the story of meeting a Palestinian who would gladly coexist with Jews as long as they were subject to Islamic rule—such rule is the natural order, this Boston-educated Arab believes. It's a prejudice, I believe, that saturates the mainstream Muslim psyche.

Yossi signs off with the advice of an older, mellower brother: "Your narrative needs more love. Not for the mullahs, but for the billions of souls over the centuries who prostrated on little embroidered prayer rugs and offered their small, unhappy lives to God's glory." Excuse me for ruining the moment, but why should so many lives continue being "small" and "unhappy," especially under a merciful God? And please don't tell me these things happen when religions are on the defensive, because even as Islam entered its golden age, lives were small and lies were big. Remember that the caliph al-Mamun trumpeted free will, yet flogged people for disagreeing with his interpretation of Islam. Not much has changed in that regard, has it?

So, I'm down to my final fair shake for Islam. Whether I leave it behind will be up to me. In another sense, though, it's up to us. What I need to see is an appetite for reform—an appetite that propels us to act.

- Will we snap out of our rites and spark our imaginations in order to free Muslims worldwide from fear, hunger, and illiteracy?
- Will we move past the superstition that we can't question the Koran? By openly asking where its verses come from, how they can be differently interpreted and why they're contradictory (as are verses in every scripture), we're not violating anything more than tribal totalitarianism.
- If my analysis is wrong, can *you* explain why no other religion is producing as many terrorist travesties and human rights transgressions in the name of God? And can you explain this without pointing fingers at everyone but Muslims?

Write me back at www.muslim-refusenik.com. I look forward to an honest discussion.

Faithfully (still),
Irshad

P.S. There's this great joke about a priest, a rabbi, and a mullah. They meet at a conference about religion, and afterwards are sitting around discussing their different faiths. The conversation turns to the topic of taboos:

> The priest says to the rabbi and the mullah, "You guys can't tell me you've never eaten pork."
>
> "Never," intones the rabbi.
>
> "Absolutely not!" insists the mullah.
>
> But the priest is skeptical. "Come on, not even once? Maybe in a fit of rebellion when you were younger?"
>
> "Okay," confesses the rabbi. "When I was young, I once nibbled bacon."
>
> "I admit it," says the mullah, laughing. "In a fit of youthful arrogance I sampled a pork chop . . ."
>
> Then the conversation turns to the priest's religious observances.
>
> "You can't tell me you've never had sex," says the mullah.
>
> "Of course not!" the priest protests. "I took a vow of chastity."
>
> The mullah and the rabbi roll their eyes. "Maybe after a few drinks?" the rabbi teases.
>
> "Perhaps, in a moment of temptation, your faith waned?" the mullah wonders.
>
> "Okay," the priest confesses. "Once, when I was drunk in seminary school, I had sexual relations with a woman."
>
> "Beats pork, huh?" say the rabbi and the mullah.

RECOMMENDED READINGS

I wanted *The Trouble with Islam Today* to feel as immediate as a conversation, so I chose not to interrupt the flow of this open letter with source notes. To see how I back up my facts and claims, please visit my Web site: www.muslim-refusenik.com.

Meanwhile, here's a sample of readings that I recommend. I heartily disagree with some of these authors, but I believe diversity of opinion is a good unto itself. This list doesn't encompass all of my research. My Web site contains plenty of other sources, including interviews, speeches, and video clips.

KEY BOOKS AND ARTICLES INCLUDE:

The Koran. N.J. Dawood, trans. London: Penguin Classics, 1956 and updated 1999.

Ajami, Fouad. *Dream Palace of the Arabs: A Generation's Odyssey.* New York: Pantheon Books, 1998.

Ali, Tariq. *Shadows of the Pomegranate Tree.* London: Chatto, 1992.

————. *The Clash of Fundamentalisms: Crusades, Jihads and Modernity.* London: Verso, 2002.

Alibhai–Brown, Yasmin. *After Multiculturalism.* London: The Foreign Policy Centre, 2000.

Armstrong, Karen. *The Battle for God: A History of Fundamentalism.* New York: Ballantine, 2000.

————. *Islam: A Short History.* London: Weidenfeld & Nicolson, 2000.

————. "Was It Inevitable?" In James F. Hoge Jr. and Gideon Rose, eds. *How Did This Happen? Terrorism and the New War.* New York: Public Affairs/Council on Foreign Relations, 2001: pp. 53–70.

Armstrong, Sally. *Veiled Threat: The Hidden Power of the Women of Afghanistan.* Toronto: Penguin, 2002.

Asfour, Gaber. "Osama Bin Laden: Financier of Intolerant 'Desert' Islam," *New Perspectives Quarterly* 18, no. 1 (Winter 2002): pp. 41–43.

Barber, Benjamin R. *Jihad vs. McWorld: How the Planet Is Both Falling Apart and Coming Together and What This Means for Democracy.* New York: Times Books, 1995.

Barlas, Asma. *"Believing Women" in Islam: Unreading Patriarchal Interpretations of the Qur'an.* Austin, Texas: University of Texas Press, 2002.

Buckman, Robert. *Can We Be Good without God? Behaviour, Belonging and the Need to Believe.* Toronto: Penguin, 2000.

Cohen, Mark. *Under Crescent and Cross: The Jews in the Middle Ages.* Princeton, N.J.: Princeton University Press, 1994.

Counts, Alex. *Give Us Credit: How Muhammad Yunus' Micro-Lending Revolution Is Empowering Women from Bangladesh to Chicago.* New York: Times Books, 1996.

Duran, Khalid. *Children of Abraham: An Introduction to Islam for Jews.* Hoboken, N.J.: Ktav Publishing House/American Jewish Committee, 2001.

El Fadl, Khaled Abou. *Speaking in God's Name: Islamic Law, Authority and Women*. Oxford, UK: Oneworld Publications, 2001.

————. With Tariq Ali, Milton Viorst, John Esposito, et al. *The Place of Tolerance in Islam*. Boston: Beacon Press, 2002. Edited by Joshua Cohen and Ian Lague for *Boston Review*.

Feiler, Bruce. *Abraham: A Journey to the Heart of Three Faiths*. New York: William Morrow, 2002.

Firestone, Reuven. *Children of Abraham: An Introduction to Judaism for Muslims*. Hoboken, N.J.: Ktav Publishing House/American Jewish Committee, 2001.

Friedman, Thomas L. *The Lexus and the Olive Tree: Understanding Globalization*. New York: Farrar, Straus Giroux, 1999.

Al-Ghazaly, [Sheikh] Muhammad. *The Future of Islam outside Its Land* (available in English at: www.ghazaly.net).

Halevi, Yossi Klein. *At the Entrance to the Garden of Eden: A Jew's Search for God with Christians and Muslims in the Holy Land*. New York: William Morrow, 2001.

Hartman, [Rabbi] David. *A Heart of Many Rooms: Celebrating the Many Voices within Judaism*. Woodstock, Vt.: Jewish Lights Publishing, 1999.

Hofmann, Murad Wilfried. *Islam: The Alternative*. Reading, UK: Garnet, 1993.

————. *Islam 2000*. Beltsville, Md.: Amana, 1997.

————. *Religion on the Rise: Islam in the Third Millennium*. Beltsville, Md.: Amana, 2001.

Hourani, Albert. *A History of the Arab Peoples*. New York: Warner Books, 1991.

Huntington, Samuel. *The Clash of Civilizations and the Remaking of World Order*. New York: Simon & Schuster, 1996.

Ignatieff, Michael. *Blood and Belonging: Journeys into the New Nationalism*. Toronto: Penguin, 1994.

Kepel, Gilles. *Jihad: The Trail of Political Islam*. Cambridge: Harvard University Press, 2002.

Lester, Toby. "What Is the Koran?" *The Atlantic Monthly* (January 1999): pp. 43–56.

Lewis, Bernard. *Semites and Anti-Semites: An Inquiry into Conflict and Prejudice*. New York: W.W. Norton, 1986.

————. *The Middle East: 2000 Years of History from the Rise of Christianity to the Present Day*. London: Weidenfeld & Nicolson, 1995.

————. *What Went Wrong? Western Impact and Middle Eastern Response*. New York: Oxford University Press, 2002.

Maalouf, Amin. *In the Name of Identity: Violence and the Need to Belong*. New York: Arcade Publishing, 2001.

Mackey, Sandra. *Passion & Politics: The Turbulent World of the Arabs*. New York: Plume, 1994.

————. *The Saudis: Inside the Desert Kingdom*. New York: W.W. Norton, 2002.

Mahbubani, Kishore. *Can Asians Think?* Toronto: Key Porter, 2001.

Makiya, Kanan. *Cruelty and Silence: War, Tyranny, Uprising, and the Arab World*. New York: W.W. Norton, 1993.

Mayer, Ann Elizabeth. *Islam and Human Rights: Tradition and Politics*. Boulder, Colo.: Westview Press, 1999.

Menocal, Maria Rosa. *The Ornament of the World: How Muslims, Jews and Christians Created a Culture of Tolerance in Medieval Spain*. Boston: Little, Brown, 2002.

Morris, Benny. *Righteous Victims: A History of the Zionist-Arab Conflict, 1881–2001*. New York: Vintage, 2001.

Naipaul, V. S. *Beyond Belief: Islamic Excursions among the Converted Peoples*. New York: Random House, 1998.

————. "Our Universal Civilization," in *The Writer and the World: Essays*. New York: Knopf, 2002: pp. 503–517

Nasrin, Taslima. *Shame: A Novel*. Amherst, N.Y.: Prometheus, 1997.

————. *Meyebela: My Bengali Girlhood*. South Royalton, Vt.: Steerforth Press, 2002.

Pearlman, Maurice. *Mufti of Jerusalem: The Story of Haj Amin el Husseini*. London: V. Gollancz, 1947.

Pipes, Daniel. *The Hidden Hand: Middle East Fears of Conspiracy*. New York: St. Martin's Press, 1996.

————. *Militant Islam Reaches America*. New York: W.W. Norton, 2002.

Ramadan, Tariq. *To Be a European Muslim*. Markfield, Leicester, UK: The Islamic Foundation, 1999.

Raphael, George. "A is for Arabs," *salon.com*. (January 8, 2002— archived).

Rubin, Barry, and Judith Colp Rubin, eds. *Anti-American Terrorism: A Documentary Reader*. New York: Oxford University Press, 2002.

Rushdie, Salman. *Step Across This Line: Collected Nonfiction 1992–2002*. New York: Random House, 2002.

Sachedina, Abdulaziz. *The Islamic Roots of Democratic Pluralism*. New York: Oxford University Press, 2001.

Sacks, [Rabbi] Jonathan. *The Dignity of Difference: How to Avoid the Clash of Civilizations*. London, New York: Continuum, 2002.

Said, Edward. *Orientalism*. New York: Vintage Books, 1979.

————. *Covering Islam: How the Media and the Experts Determine How We See the Rest of the World*. New York: Pantheon, 1981.

Salem, Ali. *A Drive to Israel: An Egyptian Meets His Neighbors*. Tel Aviv: Moshe Dayan Center for Middle Eastern and African Studies, 2001.

Sampson, Cynthia, and Douglas Johnston, eds. *Religion: The Missing Dimension of Statecraft*. New York: Oxford University Press/Center for Strategic and International Studies, 1994.

Sardar, Ziauddin. "Islam: Resistance and Reform," *New Internationalist* (May 2002): pp. 9–10.

Shehadeh, Raja. *Strangers in the House: Coming of Age in Occupied Palestine*. South Royalton, Vt.: Steerforth Press, 2002.

Taha, Mahmoud Mohamed. *The Second Message of Islam.* Syracuse, N.Y.: Syracuse University Press, 1987.

Tibi, Bassam. *The Challenge of Fundamentalism: Political Islam and the New World Disorder.* Berkeley: University of California Press, 1998.

Wadud, Amina. *Qur'an and Woman: Rereading the Sacred Text from a Woman's Perspective.* New York: Oxford University Press, 1999.

Warraq, Ibn. *Why I Am Not a Muslim.* Amherst, N.Y.: Prometheus Books, 1995.

Warraq, Ibn, ed. *Leaving Islam: Apostates Speak Out.* Amherst, N.Y.: Prometheus Books, 2003.

Wolfe, Michael, and producers of Beliefnet, eds. *Taking Back Islam: American Muslims Reclaim Their Faith.* Emmaus, Pa.: Rodale/ Beliefnet, 2002.

Ye'or, Bat. *Islam and Dhimmitude: Where Civilizations Collide.* Madison, N.J.: Farleigh Dickinson University Press, 2002.

Zachary, Pascal. *The Global Me: New Cosmopolitans and the Competitive Edge—Picking Globalism's Winners and Losers.* New York: Public Affairs, 2000.

Zakaria, Fareed. *The Future of Freedom: Illiberal Democracy at Home and Abroad.* New York: W.W. Norton, 2003.

FOR THE REALLY COMMITTED:

Ibn Rushd. *The Books of the Decisive Treatise Determining the Connection between the Law and Wisdom.* Provo, Utah: Brigham Young University Press, 2001.

To ease into the above, check out: Majid Fakhry, *Averroes: His Life, Works and Influence.* Oxford, UK: Oneworld, 2001.

Maimonides. *The Guide for the Perplexed.* Culver City, Calif.: Labyrinthos, 1989.

To ease into the above, check out: Kenneth Seeskin, *Maimonides: A*

Guide for Today's Perplexed, West Orange, N.J.: Behrman House, 1991.

Papers of the Georgetown University Center for Muslim-Christian Understanding (e.g. "The Need for Civilizational Dialogue" and "Islamists and the Challenge of Pluralism").

Proceedings of conferences sponsored by the International Council of Christians and Jews (e.g. "Convivencia: Enhancing Identity through Encounter between Jews, Christians and Muslims").

Proceedings of the Kuala Lumpur International Forum on Islam 2002.

United Nations Arab Human Development Report 2002.

World Bank Research Report: Engendering Development 2001.

REFORM-ORIENTED WEB SITES INCLUDE:

al-fatiha.net

freemuslims.org

muslim-refusenik.com

muslimwakeup.com

newislam.org

niputesnisoumises.com ("Neither Whores Nor Doormats")

secularislam.org

wluml.org ("Women Living Under Muslim Laws")

ACKNOWLEDGMENTS

This book is a lifetime in the making. To name all those who deserve my gratitude would be impossible, but a few conspirators must be singled out. Michelle Douglas, Anne Collins, Paul Michaels, and Margaret Hancock lead the pack for their gift of faith in me.

Val Ross, John Pearce, and Kendall Anderson helped me refine ideas. From there, an international platoon of research associates developed—and the ones who evolved into assistants were Samra Habib, Caroline Fernandez, and Mickey Cirak. Rick Matthews and Samuel Segev aided tremendously with fact-checking. Also vital to my education has been my work with various media, especially TVOntario, where big ideas matter.

The interventions of Frank Clarke, Amanda Sussman, and Lynsay Henderson landed me important meetings, while spirited discussions with Geraldine Sherman, Robert Fulford, Anna

Porter, Anna Morgan, Amatzia Baram, Doug Saunders, Don Habibi, and Tarek and Nargis Fatah landed me important insights. I should point out that the Fatahs disagree with my take on Palestine, as well as my charge of Muslim complicity in the Holocaust. But heated disagreement doesn't have to prevent engagement, and I look forward to the day when we'll be back on speaking terms.

It's the boost from friends during moments of flagging spirit that I most treasure. In this department, I have to mention Samantha Haywood, Adriana Salvia, Andrew Fedosov, Michel Lamoureux, Michael Savage, and the gang at Boshkung Lake. As for those who don't find their names on this brief list, they can collect on a free dinner from me. (I've mentioned only the most extravagant friends so I don't wind up in the poorhouse.) Speaking of avoiding the poorhouse, my agent, Michael Levine, and his right hand, Maxine Quigley, have my deepest appreciation.

Finally, I want to thank my mother for steeling her spine. Despite being an observant Muslim, she's never asked me not to write this book. She has, however, cautioned me not to anger God. One afternoon, while we both attended the funeral of a relative, she told me to say hello to her imam, who had flown in for the service. I offered him my hand in greeting. The imam not only refused to touch my hand, he refused to acknowledge it altogether. When I asked him why, he cited "rules." I suggested that being humane should be a higher priority than following rules. Upon hearing about this, my mother gasped to me, "I hope you weren't rude!" Mum, whether or not I've been "rude" in the preceding pages—and only you can decide for yourself—I ask of you one thing: Please don't confuse angering imams with angering God.

AFTERWORD

Confessions and Reflections of a
Muslim Refusenik

When I finished writing *The Trouble with Islam,* I didn't know what to expect. I knew that Muslims would hotly contest its contents, which is why I backed up every claim with detailed source notes on my website. (Including the notes in the pages of the book would have, among other things, killed trees needlessly—something explicitly forbidden by the Koran.)

But I was in for a surprise. "Forget the contents," protested many Muslims. "It's the title that we can't get past." To claim that there's trouble with Islam is to question the perfection of Islam, and that's off-limits. As I've heard over and over again, "There's no trouble with Islam; only with Muslims."

Please. Would these critics say that feminism is perfect; it's feminists who have twisted it? That humanism makes sense; it's the humanists who don't? That capitalism is fair; it's capitalists who aren't? Of course not. So I won't play the semantic game in this case either.

To be sure, I understand the larger point made by those who

say my title should have been *The Trouble with Muslims*. Their point is that Muslims, as human beings, commit mistakes. I agree. In this spirit, I'm willing to confess my mistakes. I should have entitled this book *The Trouble with Islam Today*. In the preceding pages I take pains to show that Islam once led the world in curiosity, creativity, and innovation. Islamic civilization shaped so much of what's known as Western pop culture; in turn, the West owes Islam a debt of gratitude for preserving and expanding knowledge.

Let me say it again. The trouble is not so much with Islam as it is with Islam today. Now that I've admitted my imperfection, I look forward to hearing from my detractors about where they've gone wrong.

And have I got detractors. Although many disapproving Muslims have engaged in thoughtful, substantive debate with me, they're far outnumbered by those who would rather shut me up altogether. I regularly receive threats through my Web site. Some of my would-be assassins emphasize the virtues of martyrdom, wanting to hurl me into the "flames of hell" in exchange for seventy-two virgins. Others simply want to know what plane I'm next boarding so they can hijack it. Somehow, I don't feel the urge to share my schedule.

There is the odd funny threat. Like the email from Basit, who began his warning to me with this question: "So you think that just because you have a mind, you should use it?" Well, when you put it that way, Basit . . . He continued, "Desist and apologize for your blaspheming ways while you still have a chance. People like you should not exist. It is no wonder there is a hell. Enjoy your short stay in this world, for God only knows what is coming for you, Irshad Manji."

A few threats have been up close and personal. At Montreal's

Trudeau Airport, a Muslim man approached my travel companion to say, "You're luckier than your friend." When she looked
at him quizzically, he turned his hand into the shape of a gun
and pulled the trigger. Like a good Canadian, she asked him to
clarify his intentions. Pointing to me, the man intoned, "She
will find out later what that means."

Still, I have never lived in fear. Not once. What Salman
Rushdie told me when I began writing the book sticks with me
as I reflect on my life since. I remember asking him why he
would encourage a young Muslim to author something that
might invite into her life the havoc that's been visited upon his.
Without any hesitation, he replied, "Because a book is more
important than a life." I laughed, thinking he'd get to the serious answer in a moment.

"Let me explain," Rushdie said. "Whenever a writer puts
out a thought, it can be disagreed with vigorously, vehemently,
even violently. But it cannot be un-thought. That is the great,
permanent gift a writer gives to this world." Words to live by.

And, for all the threats, there's good news: I'm hearing more
support, affection, and love from fellow Muslims than I thought
possible. Two groups in particular, Muslim women and young
Muslims, have flooded my website with letters of relief and
gratitude. "Tell it like it is only begins to express my feelings,"
a girl named Salimah wrote to me. "I have asked questions
for years and years about women in Islam and the Quran,
but have always received that 'Oh-Salimah-one-day-you-will-
understand' attitude. Thank you for your truth, your time in
researching the history, and your love of humanity." She signed
off with an "xo."

Muslim men who have anything positive to say almost always
identify themselves in relation to the women in their lives. I fre-

quently hear the phrase, "As a son" or "as the brother of . . ." A truly touching remark came from Anwer: "I see from the many emails posted on your site some of the venom thrown at you . . . Keep the fight up. The cause is right and just. You are a great role model for my three daughters." You hear that, mom?

Probably the most arresting letter is from a Muslim woman in Kansas. For years she was a literalist, abiding by the "supposedly God-sanctioned requirement to live on autopilot." But 9/11 and a few personal tragedies jolted her out of religious robotics. No longer will she "dampen the song in my heart" or "censor the artistic temperament."

Yet her decision to unshackle her mind has carried the cost of loneliness. As she described it, "I am more than frustrated with my insatiable appetite for dialogue in a world where the sexes are segregated, where I cannot rationalize the priority that men are given to express their archaic positions, where my choice to be a mother wife is perceived as an expectation and not a monumental sacrifice. I am, Irshad, more than a little pissed—pardon my French."

However, she went on:

"I have made at least one commitment, and one which I think would serve as a good mantra for the mission towards reform. I have decided to attach myself to ideas and ideals, regardless of whether they are espoused by those wearing turbans or yarmulkas or hijabs. My loyalties will be to ideas and ideals and never to a people, a dogma, or a culture.

Not to say that freedom is immune to corruption. A free society will foster the most brilliant of minds and souls while simultaneously allowing for the most depraved among them to exist. But using that as an argument against freedom of choice works only to sustain the lowest common human denominator.

The presence of an explicit immorality is preferable to the hypocritical depravity which results when human beings are robbed of their God-given right to choose."

For me, the tragedy of all this reform-mindedness is the silence that still engulfs it. The vast majority of Muslims who write to me in support, or who whisper "thank-you" after my public events, confide that they can't yet go public with their support. Many believe that they can't even be vocal about their own struggles with the faith today because they fear "persecution." Not ostracism. Not marginalization. Persecution—by which they mean physical retaliation against themselves and their families from fellow Muslims.

As counter-intuitive as it may sound, that's why I don't take my bodyguard everywhere I go. I used to. And security professionals have cautioned me to retain a round-the-clock bodyguard now that the book is available in Arabic and Urdu (a major language in Pakistan and India). The reality, though, is that if I'm going to have legitimacy conveying to Muslims that we can dissent with the establishment and live, I can't have a big, burly fellow looking over my shoulder. I must lead by example. So far, so good.

The relative safety with which I've debated Islam in the West—from Britain to Belgium, from Australia to Canada, from the Netherlands to the United States—convinces me that Muslims in the West have a sterling opportunity to revive ijtihad, Islam's tradition of independent reasoning. Why in the West? It's here that we already enjoy the precious freedoms to think, express, challenge, and be challenged—all without fear of state reprisal.

I'm not denying that some Muslims have been targeted for harassment, profiling, and discrimination by Western governments. I faced the same during the 1991 Gulf War, when I was marched out of a federal building for no apparent reason. But none of this negates a basic fact: that if Muslims in the West dare to ask questions about our holy book, and if we care enough to denounce human rights violations being committed under the banner of that book, we need not worry about being raped, flogged, stoned, imprisoned or executed by the state for doing so. What in God's name are Muslims in the West doing with our freedoms?

Allow me to report what a lot of young Muslims would like us to be doing: questioning ourselves as much as we question Washington. In fact, a huge motivation for having written the book came from young Muslims on Canadian and American campuses. Even before 9/11, I spoke at universities about the virtues of diversity, including diversity of opinion. After many of these speeches, it was young Muslims who emerged from the audiences, gathered at the side of the stage, chatted excitedly among themselves, and then walked over to me. "Irshad," I would hear, "we need voices such as yours to help us open up this religion of ours because if it doesn't open up, we're leaving it."

The challenge now is to transform that underground hunger for change into a visible, above-the-ground phenomenon. I'm working on it with other progressive young Muslims and non-Muslims. You can stay up-to-date on our efforts by visiting my Web site, *www.muslim-refusenik.com*.

For the moment, I relish the minor victories. There have been plenty:

- the young Muslims who convinced me to circumvent cautious Middle East publishers, get the book translated into

Arabic, and post the translation on my Web site so that they and their friends could read it without hassle or censorship;

- the teenager from Jordan who, two days after the Arabic translation went up, e-mailed to say he's starting an underground discussion group to "spread these ideas";

- the Arab-American women in Chicago who glared with contempt as I spoke but who, by the end of the evening, quietly acknowledged that "we Muslims have a lot of introspection to do";

- the Muslim couple at Oxford University who confessed that they never expected to agree with my arguments, let alone ask how they can help;

- the Jewish and Muslim students at universities across North America who sat down for the first time ever to hash out their differences;

- the atheist in France whose comfortable certainties have been shaken (though, she added, "I cannot say this to my friends because they would stone me!");

- the Australian-Muslim man who works at the Canberra Islamic Centre and informed me that my book would be on sale there because "it's about bloody time that a new generation of Muslims raised in the West raised their voices against the oppressor, who [oppresses] in the name of Islam and conformity";

• the Muslim girls from Saudi Arabia who told an irate elder at a New York event that "now is exactly the time for a book like this";

• and the hijab-wearing woman in Atlanta who said she's so upset by what I've written that it inspires her to "hit the books and write my own." If she's reading this, she should know that my offer to introduce her to my publisher still stands.

My favorite story, though, has to do with my mother's evolution. Two weeks after the book came out, she phoned to tell me that she'd just been to the mosque for the first time since the book's release. She girded herself for criticism—and got lots of it. But, she added, several congregants also approached her to affirm that "what Irshad is saying needs to be said." Their comments comforted her that I'm not a self-hating Muslim waging a vendetta against Islam. (I only regret that she needed social approval to confirm that.)

Two more weeks later, I visited my mum during a book tour. Into my suitcase, she slipped a card that I found only upon arriving home. The front of the card read, "Bravo!" And inside my mum wrote, among other things, "You go girl!"

It means the world that my intention has the blessing of this utterly devout Muslim, whatever the consequences for me, for her, or for our faith.

—Irshad Manji, Toronto
February 2005

READING GROUP GUIDE

1. Irshad Manji writes her book in the form of an open letter. Do you like this approach? In what ways do you find this style successful or unsuccessful?

2. One of the biggest debates about this book is its title. Irshad has responded to the controversy by clarifying that the trouble is with Islam "today." Does this change add balance to her argument?

3. Did you check Irshad's sources on her Web site? If so, what did you think about this tactic? Did it engage you to go beyond the book?

4. Irshad has been criticized for challenging her fellow Muslims at a time when fear of Islam is rampant. Is there ever a good time to write a book like this?

5. Irshad defines herself as a Muslim refusenik. What does she mean by this statement and do you feel it is valid?

6. Irshad shows that the Koran contains passages that are both hostile and friendly toward women. So why does the public focus on the Koran's negative verses? Is it the media, the mullahs, or the silent moderates who should take responsibility for Islam's antifemale image?

7. Throughout the book, Irshad emphasizes ijtihad, Islam's lost tradition of independent thinking. Why, according to her, did ijtihad die in much of the Muslim world?

8. Historically, Irshad claims, the rift between Muslims and Jews started well before the state of Israel existed. What does she see as the source of the rift?

Continued on next page

St. Martin's Griffin

Reading Group Guide

9. Irshad distinguishes between religion and culture, saying that Arab culture places too strong a hold on the way Islam is practiced. What are her examples and do you agree with them?

10. Irshad's campaign to revive ijtihad starts by economically empowering women in the Islamic world. Does this sound like a realistic solution? What can you do to support it?

11. Irshad quotes Rev. Martin Luther King Jr., who said that every society needs people to create nonviolent tension and jolt others out of moral complacency. Is Islamic reform the new global civil rights movement? If so, what role does Irshad envision non-Muslims playing in this movement?

12. Do you share Irshad's suspicions about interfaith dialogue?

13. What value does Irshad find in religion? Are dissidents like her entitled to "keep the faith" or is religion meant to be a set of rules by which you have to play if you're going to stay?

14. At the end of the book, Irshad tells us that a friend felt her tough love approach to Muslims needs more love. Does it?

15. In her acknowledgments, Irshad says that "despite being an observant Muslim, [my mother] never asked me not to write this book. She has, however, cautioned me not to anger God." If your child were to write a controversial critique of your religion, what would you advise him or her?

For more reading group suggestions visit
www.stmartins.com/smp/rgg.html

St. Martin's Griffin